"Stand at the crossroads and look;
ask for the ancient paths,
ask where the good way is,
and walk in it,
and you will find rest for your souls."

Jeremiah 6:16

The Good Way

Walking an Old Road to a New Life

Ronald K. Ottenad

THE GOOD WAY
Walking an Old Road to a New Life

Copyright © 2015 by Ronald K. Ottenad

All rights reserved. This book or any portion thereof may not be reproduced or used in any manner whatsoever without the express written permission from Rooted Soul Ministries Inc., 3653 Hackett Ave. Long Beach, CA 90808

ISBN 978-0-9864325-0-7

Cover design by Joshua Coffey
Cover Image: Rural Countryside Road Through Fields With Wheat, © Can Stock Photo Inc., ryhor

Scripture taken from the HOLY BIBLE, NEW INTERNATIONAL VERSION®. NIV®. Copyright © 1973, 1978, 1984 by International Bible Society. Used by permission of Zondervan. All rights reserved worldwide.

Printed in the United States of America

First Printing, 2015

DEDICATION

For my wife, Tammie,
who not only gives me the freedom to walk,
but is always by my side.

For my children, Michael and Kristen,
who bring joy and laughter to life,
and are my inspiration to continue to grow.

For those who could envision
what God was giving birth to during this season
and who were willing to partner in this project.

For those who gave above and beyond any
reasonable expectation to make this journey possible:
Catherine Antone
Dana Davis
Mark Holmes
Jeff Megorden
Ron and Anne Ottenad
Susie Overton
Donna and Al Penrod
Christine Lee Smith
And Judy and Gene TenElshof

Finally, for those who walked with me,
your presence on this journey was a gift.
I treasure you all.

CONTENTS

1.	Where it All Began	1
2.	Learning to Walk	13
3.	When You Choose	23
4.	Suspicions	33
5.	Being With	45
6.	Waiting	55
7.	Becoming Family	69
8.	Letting Go	81
9.	Created Space	95
10.	Wilderness and Stones	109
11.	The Fall	121
12.	Compassion and Comfort	133
13.	Lavish Love	145
14.	A New Pace	157
15.	Blessings	167
16.	Final Steps	175
17.	Santiago	187
18.	Going Home	197
	Epilogue: Rest Assured	
	Appendix: The Significance of the Camino de Santiago	
	Notes	

Chapter One

WHERE IT ALL BEGAN

I stepped off the bus and walked down the street to the stone arch leading to the old city of St. Jean Pied de Port. The people I passed on the streets were dressed in the latest hiking fashions and moisture wicking fabrics, appearing out of place in this medieval village. Yet pilgrims just like them—albeit in different clothes—have been walking these well-trodden byways for more than 1,000 years as they made their way along the Camino de Santiago.

Looking up, the blue sky was dotted with billowing white clouds. I could not tell if they were the leading edge of a storm front or the tail end of a system that had just passed through. Maybe both. Whatever the case, they provided richness to the heavens and a beautiful backdrop for an afternoon of exploring this small town. As I did so, I would also be mentally preparing myself for crossing the Pyrenees Mountains the next day. In the morning, I would take my first steps toward Santiago on the cobblestone streets that were now beneath my feet.

Some people assume that St. Jean Pied de Port is the beginning of the Camino, but this is not correct. It is the main jumping off point for many who choose to walk the Camino Frances, which is only one of the routes to Santiago. I met people along the way who started in Burgos, Leon, Sarria and many other towns that dot this route. There were others who began in cities and towns before St. Jean. One man I met had been walking nearly a month and a half before arriving in the city many mistakenly consider as the starting point of the Camino. Setting out from his home, it took him longer to get to St. Jean than it would for him to walk from there to Santiago. He was indicative of the majority of the pilgrims who have walked the Camino de Santiago throughout the centuries. They did not take a plane, train, or bus to a starting point. They simply stepped out their front door and began their journey toward Santiago.

This is why the Camino Frances is only one route leading to Santiago. Spain, and indeed all of Europe, is covered with a web of paths that lead to Santiago de Compostela. The cathedral there is believed to be the final resting place for the bones of St. James, the disciple of Christ who brought the gospel to this part of the world. The pilgrimage to this place was one of the three recognized by the church in medieval times, the other two being Rome and Jerusalem. The journey to Santiago did not begin in a set location; it began right where you were and with a stirring in your heart that beckoned you to walk.

Ironically, I was not even present when my Camino journey began. My wife, Tammie, was beginning classes at a church that had taken much of what I had learned in my spiritual formation graduate degree program and adapted it into a class for its congregation. On the first night, after the lecture, the participants broke into cohort groups to discuss and apply what they were learning. Their first experience would be an exercise in group spiritual direction. It is a way of praying for one another, but with a different process than is typically followed. Rather than asking someone what they would like prayer for and then talking to God about it, the group would allow a person to share a situation of concern and then the members would turn to God and listen. The Lord might bring to their mind a passage of Scripture, an encouraging word, lines from a song, or a mental picture. They would then share what they believed God had revealed to them through prayer. Being a new format for most people, it was probably a bit uncomfortable and even a little risky. The room was filled with silence as they each waited to see who would be brave enough to jump in.

Tammie privately told God she was not going to share unless the room was silent five minutes, because as a pastor's wife, she feared this would not be a safe environment. She watched the clock. The room remained silent. Five minutes passed and still no one had spoken. She could feel the Holy Spirit pressing on her heart and so she finally began with the words, "I have something to share."

She told them about the financial situation at our church, where I served as executive pastor (second in line to the senior pastor and responsible for overseeing church staff). Our church had weathered the financial crisis of 2008, and spending cuts and belt-tightening had done as much as they could. But by 2012, when Tammie finally shared, church finances posed a severe problem. Year-end giving had not been as robust as leadership had hoped, and now we found ourselves in a financial pinch. The elders had told the congregation that if giving did not increase, staff layoffs would be needed to solve our financial crisis. Everyone on staff wondered if they would be the one who would be let go. All Tammie told them in the moment was that she felt concerned about the possible layoffs and it was heavy on her heart.

When Tammie finished sharing with the group, the leader asked the members to take the situation to God in prayer. They were given time to sit in silence and listen on my wife's behalf. After a few minutes, the leader asked if anyone had anything they felt like God wanted them to share.

A woman began to share tentatively: "I saw your husband. He was standing and the light of Christ was shining down on him. Then he was removed." She was emphatic about this point. "He was removed, and standing behind him was someone who had a cloak covering his head. The man wearing the cloak represents a person or group who is in authority over your husband."

The woman went on to say, "The light of Christ remained upon your husband even after he was removed, but the person who was standing behind him had the hood of the cloak removed and they were exposed." The woman admitted she was not sure what it all meant, but that is what came to her in the silence.

Others in the circle also shared what they felt God had revealed, but the image this lady painted seemed to resonate most with Tammie. She could not wait to share with me what had taken place.

Tammie was surprised to find me at home when she arrived. It was the second Monday of the month, the night of our regular elder meetings. For the better part of the previous twenty years, I had spent every second Monday with the senior pastor and the elders. Our meetings would

Where It All Began

often go quite late, and to find me at home before ten o'clock was unusual. For only the second time since I had been attending these meetings, I was asked to leave early. The senior pastor said he wanted to discuss some matters with the elders by himself. I thought he wanted to give the elders an update on his personal life in private. This seemed reasonable to me, so I left without giving it much thought.

However, my early departure seemed much more foreboding when Tammie walked through the door and announced, "I think we are the ones who are going to be let go." At that time, we were both on staff at the church, and it was hard to imagine that she would stay on if I were laid off. We were not sure exactly what would come next, but we both sensed something significant was underway.

We had no choice but to wait and pray. Though we knew nothing for sure, what the woman had shared seemed consistent with the way the senior pastor and elder chairman were acting. In the week prior to Tammie's prayer experience, I had conversations with both men. I had sensed something was in the works that would impact me directly and asked each of them to shoot straight with me.

Two weeks later, I would find out neither one of them chose to do so.

* * *

It was a Thursday, and most of the staff were attending a half day conference. Since I had end-of-month financial statements to complete, I had stayed at the office. Being two weeks since the last elder meeting, the chairman sent an email containing the minutes so all attendees could review and approve them. As I scrolled down the page, I came to the point in the meeting when I had been asked to leave. Rather than the senior pastor sharing about his personal life, he made the recommendation to remove me from my position and place someone else in my role. The minutes stated that he was making the proposal in order to realign the pastoral staff with their individual gifts and passions in ministry.

Obviously, including this information in meeting minutes for all to see was an unfortunate oversight. But there it was. For me, this was a devastating way to find out about the proposed change. It was even harder to absorb the fact the men I had worked alongside and trusted would get this far through the process without talking to me. Receiving the news would have been tough at any time, but being told personally and beforehand would have been honoring to the relationships we shared and my many years of service and leadership. After all, this was the body of Christ, not a business. It was a family, not an organization.

In truth, I felt hurt and betrayed.

What followed was a day of conversations, first with Tammie. I showed her what I had discovered in the email. It did not take long for us to remember the vision that had been shared with her. I was indeed being removed. I then met with my best friend, who took me to lunch and allowed me to vent all my hurt, frustration, and anger. That afternoon I met with the senior pastor and later that evening with the elder chairman.

As you can imagine, those were uncomfortable and painful discussions. What was said in them, in the end, was not nearly as important as the reality I was being invited on a journey, even if I did not fully recognize it in the moment. I could not control the circumstances suddenly swirling around me. I could not control the decisions being made that would affect my family and me so profoundly. All I could do was choose how I would go about walking through it.

* * *

Within a few days of receiving the email, I also received an invitation from the Lord. If you have had any practice of reading Scripture over time, you have probably had the experience of reading a verse multiple times without having it reveal anything remarkable to you—only to have it speak to you powerfully and personally at the very moment you need it most. This was my experience. I had been reading through the book of Jeremiah when I came to chapter 6, verse 16. I knew in an instant it had something to say to me about how I was to walk through this journey. The passage says, "This is what the Lord says: 'Stand at the crossroads and look; ask for the ancient paths, ask where the good way is, and walk in it, and you will find rest for your souls.'"

The crossroads I found myself at was extremely significant. I had spent my entire adult life at the church where I had served. I started attending there as a college student. I met Tammie there, and we were married in its sanctuary. My children were raised in that church from birth. It was the only close community they ever knew outside of family. In many ways, it was their extended family. I had served this body of believers long before I was ever invited to become part of staff. I had always felt a sense of calling to serve there—not just a "hired hand" to fill a position. I had loved my role and the people I served.

THE GOOD WAY

Now, all of this was in jeopardy, and indeed it eventually would be taken from us. I did not know at the time how events would unfold; all I knew was that I had to decide how I would navigate the crossroads where I found myself. It is the choices I made while standing at this crossroads that would eventually lead me to walk the Camino de Santiago.

* * *

While walking one morning along my normal route in the park near our house, the concerns on my heart and the Camino de Santiago became intertwined. I had read about the Camino in a book called *The Way is Made by Walking: A Pilgrimage Along the Camino de Santiago* by Arthur Paul Boars. His insights about his experience, especially how he talked about his faith with those he met intrigued me. I told Tammie she should read it and even hinted that someday maybe we could make the walk. She didn't pick up on my hint but did mention that I might like a movie which had come out about the Camino called *The Way*. Thanks to Amazon.com, the movie arrived a few days later. I now had images to put to the words I had read in the book. The idea of walking the Camino intrigued me even more. This was a year before the transitions began at church, and the idea of walking the Camino had been put on the back burner. That is, until that morning in the park.

I had been meditating on Jeremiah 6:16, pondering what God had been teaching me since the day I had received the email containing the elder minutes. I contemplated the crossroads where I was still standing. I thought about the ancient path.

When we find ourselves at a crossroads, our initial

reaction is to try and determine which road will lead us to where we are supposed to go. We can stand at the intersection trying to discern which direction we are to move, afraid if we make the wrong choice we will end up somewhere we do not wish to be, or somewhere where we are afraid God will not be. We fear if we make the wrong turn, we may move away from Him, or worse yet He may abandon us. He may leave us to walk down that road alone, and our circumstance will go from bad to worse. I was not immune from these thoughts. I had trusted the men I served with would shoot straight with me, and they didn't. Circumstances in our lives like this can leave us with many questions: Why did God allow this to happen? Would He also allow me to turn down a wrong road? How far down it would He let me go before He intervened? What would I lose if I choose the wrong path?

By God's grace, I have not spent the majority of my time thinking about these questions, though I must confess they do come back to me from time to time. When they do, I ask God to give me the kind of vision which would allow me to set them aside so I can look for the answer to a different set of questions. I want to know where I can find the ancient path. I long for God to help me answer the question, "Where is the good way?" From the very beginning of this journey, I understood it was by finding the "good way" I would also find rest for my soul, which had been subjected to such hurt, pain, and betrayal.

While thinking and praying through these things, a connection began to form in my mind. In the book I read and the movie I watched, I learned when you pass others as you walk along the Camino, whether they are fellow pilgrims or locals who live along the way, you greet one another with the phrase, "Buen Camino." This can literally be translated "Good Way." I knew I had been traveling on a path over the past two years and had been seeking to understand what it meant to walk in it as you would the ancient path or good way.

This had been an internal journey involving my mind, emotions, and will. Now I began to wonder how a physical journey on the Camino might mirror the spiritual journey I had been on. What voice might walking the Camino give to what I had been living and experiencing? How would the physical journey help me to understand the path I had already been walking along in my heart? What insight might it give me about letting go and moving on?

Over this season of transition, there have been times when Tammie and I have returned to the picture given to us during her group-prayer experience. Over time, it became quite clear to us what removal meant. What has not been as apparent is who was represented by the person standing behind me, veiled in a cloak, and who is to be exposed. To be honest, I can get caught up in trying to figure it out, but most days I am content to leave it in the hands of my heavenly Father. In some ways, it does not matter who it represents. Knowing would not restore what has been lost, nor would it bring healing. In fact, speculation can take our focus off what I think is the real reason God allowed the picture to be shared with Tammie. His light is shining upon us, and He will not depart from us. Our hope comes from knowing whose face is shining upon us as we stand at the crossroads seeking to discern the good way.

The Thursday after receiving the email from the elders, before most people knew what was going on in our life, Tammie received a call from a good friend who was at a choir concert. She explained that the director had led the choir and the audience in a time of worship. It was the kind of deep worship where you stop thinking about what is going on around you and are ushered into the presence of God. In that moment, Tammie's friend said God gave her a picture and she felt she needed to share it: she saw our family standing in the rain, but it was not water that was falling—it was golden light. The mercy of God rained down upon us. She did not understand all of what was going on in our life, but she knew God wanted us to know His mercy would shower down upon us. This golden light, this light of Christ shining upon us, became the light by which we would find and walk in the good way.

Chapter Two

LEARNING TO WALK

At the albergue in St. Jean, I shared a room with an Italian couple that did not speak English. I didn't speak Italian, so except for a few pleasant smiles and gestures we did not share much except for the excitement of what the next morning would bring and perhaps a bit of nervousness about how the first day of walking would go. If you begin walking in St. Jean Pied de Port, you do not ease into the Camino. Your first day is one of the hardest you will face on the entire journey. You travel twenty-five kilometers (15.5 miles) and climb 1,240 meters (4,068 feet) before descending 469 meters (1,538 feet) into Roncevaux. Stories abound of people who struggle over this pass, even on the good days. Many recommend cutting it short with a stay in Orisson to split the climb into two days. There are also those who say it is not as bad as people make it out to be, and anyone in reasonable shape will be able to walk it without much difficulty. The truth is the only way to discover which camp you will fall into is to walk it yourself.

As I lay in bed, I pondered the definition of "reasonable shape" and wondered if I trained adequately.

THE GOOD WAY

The forecast said there was a significant chance of rain. How would this affect our ability to make it over the pass? Would we be forced to take the alternative route? If so, what would we miss? These kinds of questions along with the rhythmic snoring of the Italian man sleeping in the bunk next to me kept me from settling into a deep, restful sleep. In just a few short hours, the questions rolling around in my mind would begin to be answered.

One thing was for certain: I knew I would not begin walking alone. I chose that particular albergue because it required its guests to take part in a communal meal. It was an opportunity to meet people before you began walking and, hopefully, help you to start forming what would become a "Camino family." The twenty people staying there were from all over the world, speaking a variety of languages. But with several people translating, we were able to discover each other's names, countries, and reason for setting out on this journey. I shared Jeremiah 6:16 and told them I was seeking the ancient path, the good way, and rest for my soul. The reasons others were walking were as diverse as the countries they came from. A few were returning after having walked the Camino before, some were hoping the experience would help to clarify their life direction, others sought a connection with God, and there were those who simply were there for the adventure of it all. Despite the many reasons for coming, there was a sense of camaraderie among the strangers who were now sharing a meal and would soon begin this journey together toward Santiago.

As we ate, we got to know one another even better, sharing a bit about our lives back home and our hopes and expectations for the coming days. Several of us decided that we should not begin alone and agreed to meet outside the albergue after breakfast and set out together. That afternoon, I had arrived in St. Jean alone and I had spent the day exploring the village by myself. Most of the people sitting around the table had come in much the same way. Now, midway through our first meal, we were already beginning to form the relationships that would become significant threads woven through each of our individual experiences.

***

The next morning, I was one of the first people at the breakfast table. I finished quickly, too excited to savor the meal. I then waited anxiously for my fellow pilgrims who had decided to begin the journey together. I was in a hurry—an urgency I would have to intentionally address in a few days—but I did not recognize it yet. For now, I just wanted to get moving.

It was seven o'clock by the time we had assembled outside in the street directly across from the pilgrim's office. With packs on our backs, smiles on our faces, hope in our hearts, and a bit of drizzle falling from the sky, we set out. We did not even get to the end of the village before we made our first stop. It was apparent the drizzle was not simply a morning mist. It was beginning to fall heavier now. We all stopped to dress ourselves in rain gear before we began the long climb up into the Pyrenees.

As for my question about the difficulty of the first day, by the end of the day I agreed it was a strenuous walk. It was made even more so because of the rain. At the beginning, the light rain was a blessing. We were walking on paved roads, climbing a steep incline, and the rain brought cooling relief. By midday, however, we moved off the road and onto dirt paths—actually mud tracks that were often covered in several inches of water. The rain fell much harder. While my poncho mostly did its job and kept the rain out, it also kept in the perspiration being put off by my body. So whether because of rain or sweat, I was drenched. My shoes and clothes were soaked.

As difficult as the climb up the pass was, the decent into Roncevaux was even harder. With each step came the risk of slipping and falling in the mud. The steep, slippery descent punished our knees and forced us to stay mentally focused on each step. One of the primary reasons people do not finish the Camino is due to injuries sustained on downhill parts of the trail. The thought of sustaining such an injury and having to end my trek caused me to move slowly and deliberately down the mountain.

Just before I arrived at the day's destination, Brant and Litsa passed me on the trail. These were two friends who had met on the Camino the previous summer and were walking the first leg of the Camino together this year. They had been at the albergue the night before, and we shared a cup of coffee midway through the day as we made our way to Roncevaux. They had stayed longer at the rest stop and were now passing me on the trail. Brant was a great help in the early stages of the Camino because he had walked this way before. They assured me as they passed that we did not have far to go before we arrived. I followed behind them and watched as Litsa slipped on some light-colored mud on a steep section of the trail. I made a mental note of the spot so I could avoid it and then proceeded to slip and fall in the very same place. We cleaned our shoes off in the small river that was flowing just before we got to the monastery and made our way to our rooms for the night. I felt spent. My knees were sore,

Learning to Walk

my feet hurt, and I was cold.

In the early stages of the Camino, this is how you feel. Your body is adjusting to walking anywhere from thirteen to twenty-two miles per day. You are carrying everything you need on your back and dealing with whatever elements the weather decides to throw at you. I remember thinking, *I wonder if I will be able to actually keep this up for eight hundred kilometers (five hundred miles).*

The weather, terrain, and distance are not the only things travelers have to combat. For many, they have to combat their own bodies or their own will. It is said that people's bodies will speak and let them know what it needs. Wise pilgrims listen to their bodies. But not everyone is willing to take note of what their body might be telling them. Many approach the Camino as something to be conquered or measured against. They come to it and want to prove they can master it. You spot these people in the early days of the walk because they often suffer from injuries such as tendonitis or severe blisters. By the time we arrived in Pamplona, only three days into our trip, some people were already dropping off the Camino because injuries sustained in the first three days had made it impossible to walk. I watched people speed past me early on, deciding they were going to cover forty kilometers (twenty-five miles) in a day, only to pass them a few days later because they had to rest for a day because they pushed too hard, too fast.

While in Zubiri—our stop at the end of day two—I met a woman named Karen. This was Karen's third time walking the Camino. Both her experience and her demeanor made her one of those people who exude wisdom. I told her how the walk between Roncevaux and Zubiri had been pretty rough on my knees and how slow I felt coming down the mountain. In kindness, she complimented my progress and encouraged me to walk at my own pace. She then shared some wise words that stuck with me for the rest of the Camino: "If you do not humble yourself to the Camino, the Camino will humble you." That's exactly what we had seen in more than a few people who began the journey thinking they had something to prove, wanting to somehow conquer the Camino. Rather than whipping it into submission, they were humbled, betrayed by tendons, blisters, or knees.

***

Like the Camino, the beginning of the transition out of my church position was the hardest part. There was no easing into it. I felt as if a bomb had exploded, and I knew that nothing would ever be the same. The body of believers I served was our family, our home. The people who made it up were surrogate aunts, uncles, and grandparents to my children. The transition was not just a job change—it was whole-life change.

Once the dust had settled from the explosion caused by the errant email, the church leaders came back and asked me to consider taking a different position on staff. It would be a demotion, but the leadership felt like it would allow them to move in the direction they wanted to go and allow me to focus on areas I was passionate about. As they explained it, the new job would be about half of my old job, with the remaining hours spent on three new areas of ministry. They then asked me to draft a job description for it. Once the senior pastor and elders had tweaked the description I had given them, they asked me if I would accept the new job.

Learning to Walk

At this point, it was time to sit down with my children and explain what was taking place. I took my son, Michael, out to dinner and told him the whole story and explained what I was being asked to do. If you know any children who have grown up in a ministry home, you may have noticed they possess wisdom and maturity about church and how it works that is often beyond their years. I first discovered this when Michael was in junior high school. Tammie and I were talking in semi-code about a ministry issue. He was playing video games on the computer, seemingly unaware we were in the room. When Tammie asked me a question, Michael turned around and gave us his opinion about what we should do. He spoke with such wisdom and clarity that it was apparent this was not the first time he had been eavesdropping.

When I finished sharing with Michael everything about my situation, he spoke with the same wisdom and clarity he had demonstrated before. He told me that despite the changes the church was making, things were not going to get better. In fact, he felt things would get worse. He encouraged me to get out now before it became more painful. He went on to tell me several types of jobs he thought I would be particularly good at. I was speechless. How could a twenty-year-old see with such precision and come to such conclusions? All those years of listening and observing, I suppose.

I told Michael he was probably right and if I were just concerned about being right or protecting myself, I would pick up my ball and go home. But what if God was doing something bigger here? I explained I am more concerned about *who I am becoming* than *what I do*. I pulled out my Bible and read a passage from Philippians:

THE GOOD WAY

> "In your relationships with one another, have the same mindset as Christ Jesus: Who, being in very nature God, did not consider equality with God something to be used to his own advantage; rather, he made himself nothing by taking the very nature of a servant, being made in human likeness. And being found in appearance as a man, he humbled himself by becoming obedient to death — even death on a cross!" (2:5-8).

I explained how we often read this inspiring passage in church, but we are not usually eager to live it out. We would much rather take control, master our circumstances, and prove our worth. But what if we took seriously the admonition to take on the same mindset of Christ and chose to humble ourselves? I asked Michael, "What if this is not simply an offer by the elders to do a different job, but an invitation from my heavenly Father to enter the school of humility? Should I be willing? Would I be willing?" I explained that in order to be humbled, I might have to risk humiliation. My desire was to look beyond my circumstance to the person I would be as I walked through this transition. I would not call what was happening good, but I was willing to risk trusting in a good God who has the capacity to redeem all things.

The first step in humbling myself was to invite others into the process. The decision to accept or reject the position being offered was a choice Tammie and I were unwilling to make alone. Our hearts were too attached to the people we served and ministered alongside. We were also deeply hurt and knew there was potential for our decision to be more of a reaction than a prayerful response. We understood our choice would impact everything, and we needed help in discerning the will of God. Because of all of these factors, we asked people we knew and trusted to participate in seeking the Lord's guidance.

We gathered together a variety of people who we trusted to offer honest insights which were free from emotional reaction. After Tammie and I shared our story and the decisions before us, we asked the people to spend time in silence, asking God if there was anything He desired to speak through them. We requested that they listen for individual guidance for Tammie and myself. The common theme which emerged as they shared what God impressed upon them regarding Tammie centered on her being able to have her own voice. This was something she was not always able to express because of being married to the executive pastor. They also felt strongly that Tammie had the freedom to choose to stay on staff or resign.

For me, someone presented the image of being on a large ship headed for a storm. The person felt like I was being invited to go below deck and be with the people while the storm raged above. The other image shared was that of being "unglued." Whether this was in order to grow at my church or to be removed from it, the person did not know. The individual felt as if this was part of the process of loosening the bonds I had with this community. No one sensed a freedom for me to leave at that point.

God would speak even more clearly to Tammie some months later. She had spent a day sharing about her ministry with the man who took over my role and who was now in charge of staff. She told him how the past three years of her ministry had felt like the most spiritually fruitful of her seventeen-plus years in children's ministry. She shared the story of the fifth-grade student who had also noticed the difference and explained it by saying, "I feel like we used to learn about God—now I feel like we are actually getting to know God." Tammie showed this man the prayer journals the children had written in. They were evidence of the depth at which they were encountering God and the ways their lives were being transformed. It was exciting for her to be able to share how the Holy Spirit had been working.

A week later, he met with Tammie once again to give input on how he wanted her to move forward in her ministry. He told her he wanted her to develop a marketing strategy for children's ministry and have more events to draw people in and increase the numbers. Tammie's heart sank. She felt as if he had missed the point of everything she had shared. Still, she went home and began putting together the plan he had requested. She is a strategic thinker, so putting together this kind of ministry plan would not be difficult. But she also knew it would not produce the kind of growth she had seen in the children over the previous three years. An hour into creating what her new boss had asked for, she heard God say, "You do not have to do this. You have the freedom to step away." The next morning she turned in her resignation.

Meanwhile, I accepted the position I had been offered. I chose to willingly enter the school of humility, to go below deck and be with the people as the storm raged above me, and to allow the process of ungluing to do its work. Like the pilgrim who listens to what his body tells him as he walks the Camino, all I could do in the present moment was listen to what the Spirit seemed to be saying and respond accordingly.

What I did not recognize when I made my choice was I would be humbled even further by the men who led the church. My education had just begun.

Chapter Three

WHEN YOU CHOOSE

One of the most common questions I am asked by people is, "When did you decide to walk the Camino?" If they know anything about the progression of my story, they may assume it was after reading *The Way is Made by Walking*. They may think, like many of the Americans I met along the Camino, the decision was made after seeing the movie *The Way*. If the person was one of the supporters of my Kickstarter project, which is how I funded the journey, they may just think the decision was made when I put together my proposal and invited others to partner with me. Some may assume the choice was made only after my project was fully funded. The truth is they would all be right. The decision to walk the Camino was a daily decision. It not only encompassed every movement toward the journey before I began to walk, but it also included every morning I swung my feet out of bed in whatever albergue I happened to be sleeping in, put on my shoes, and set out the door to walk another day.

During training, I had to make an active choice to leave my house and walk. There were days I had planned on walking much longer distances than I would normally cover in a day, with the intention of building up the stamina necessary for each day on the Camino. When I awoke on those mornings, I would often find my will fighting against what I knew was best for the preparation of my body. The battle took place in my mind. I found myself trying to justify why walking a shorter distance would be better for my training than the longer miles I had planned. Maybe I would feel a bit of soreness in my legs and make an excuse to myself such as, *I don't want to risk injuring myself just before I leave.* I tried to convince myself that walking longer distances would not really help build endurance and was just a waste of time. After all, there were so many other things I needed to do before I departed for forty days. I would ask myself, *Wouldn't my time be spent in a better way than walking for four or five hours on a Saturday?* When you are planning on walking five hundred miles in thirty-two days the answer is no, but that did not prevent my distorted desire for comfort from trying to convince myself otherwise. The arguments against walking that I would wrestle with might originate in will, body, or mind. It was a great temptation to allow whichever one was trying to deceive myself to win the argument and put off the long training day.

The thought of not being able to complete the distances I had mapped out for each day—or worse, not finishing the Camino at all—kept me from giving in to the desires waging war with what I knew to be true. The best way to prepare to walk is to walk. The best way to prepare to walk long distances is to walk long distances. The mornings I had scheduled to train for the Camino became an opportunity to train in something much more necessary than the ability for my body to endure long distances. They were a chance to train my will to choose to walk, even when my mind and body had no desire to do so. In exercising my ability to make these choices, I was conditioning myself to choose to walk each morning while in Spain.

The ability to make these choices is one of the most important things you will bring to the Camino. It is also the most important capacity you will bring as you navigate the crossroads of your life. You cannot get to where God is leading in one day's journey. It will be a series of days and even seasons linked together that will enable you to arrive at the destination intended by God.

Not long after the beginning of my journey, I sat with a group of fellow pilgrims talking about the day's walk and what our experience had been thus far. One of them told the story of a man whom I did not yet have the fortune to meet, nor would I, because one day into his Camino he decided he was done. The first night, after walking only one day, he announced that he was finished. He said he had discovered what he had been looking for on the Camino and had no reason to continue. That's possible, I guess. Even so, there could've been many other things to discover along the way. Imagine all the money spent and months of planning that went into this fellow's setting out on the Camino. I cannot help but wonder if the question he asked himself was, "Do I have it within me to walk this path?" Maybe, after the first day, he had discovered the answer, and it was no.

I believe the choice to walk the Camino is made each and every day as you move toward it, as you walk upon it, and even as you return home and endeavor to continue to live in the rhythm you discovered while walking. It was much the same with my decision to walk in the path of humility set before me at my church. I wish it was a one-

and-done decision, but it wasn't. It was a choice to be made every time an opportunity for humility was presented. I had a choice when asked to train the man who was taking my position. I had a choice after I was stripped of authority but still held responsible for the outcomes of the areas I continued to oversee. I had a choice when decisions were made in my area of ministry without consulting me. At times it felt as if each day presented me with another opportunity to choose humility.

All of these circumstances, and others like them, pointed to the fact I had gone from being at the center of what was taking place at the church to being pushed to the margin. Like progress on the Camino, the changes at the church were incremental and progressive. I was not pushed to the outside of the circle in one fell swoop. With each movement toward the new reality also came the opportunity to choose again to walk the path of humility. I was learning what it meant to take on the same attitude we find in Christ Jesus, who humbled Himself. It was painful and difficult.

Honestly, I wished it had been different. I surely would have preferred to be in a place where I felt cared for, valued and esteemed. I would like to have continued to be included in discussions and decisions being made rather than simply being informed. But I knew if I wanted to fulfill the ultimate desire of my heart—to become like the one I follow—I had to get up each morning and push past my desires for safety, comfort and control which were tempting me to walk in any path but the one I had been invited into, and choose humility.

A passage from Isaiah helped me to learn how to walk in humility: "In repentance and rest is your salvation, in quietness and trust is your strength" (30:15). Some translations replace the word *repentance* with *returning*: "In returning and rest is your salvation." The nation of Israel had been rebellious and unwilling to hear the instruction of the Lord. They desired for their prophets to tell them what they wanted to hear rather than what was true about whom they had become. They did not trust in God and the word He had given; instead, they lived in ways that contradicted what God expected of them. The people of Israel thought they would be able to make themselves secure. In this passage, however, God says it is in recognizing how wrong they have been, turning from this path, and entering rest they will discover salvation and security.

My first move in learning to walk in humility was to ask, "Is there anything I need to repent and return from?" I had worked at the church for a long time. The transition I was going through forced me to evaluate if I had been part of the dysfunction of which I was now victim. I know how easy it is for our own minds to justify our actions and convince us we have not done anything wrong. I also understand how quickly we can fall into the trap of believing we no longer have any value. Because of the potential of these personal deceptions, I decided to invite those I had worked with in the past to speak into these areas.

I began to approach men I had served with—those no longer on staff—to ask for input on my leadership style and the environment of our church. Some of the things they shared were encouraging and affirming; other things were hard to hear. Some comments related directly to me; other things related to the culture of the church. I endeavored to listen without defensiveness. When appropriate and necessary, I asked for forgiveness. Each one of them was gracious enough to extend it. My final question was always the same: "If down the road there was the opportunity to work together again, would you?" They all answered yes. Their response went a long way to helping me enter rest.

I did not leave my exploration of my leadership with them. I also spent many months asking the Holy Spirit to help me see the things I needed to admit and turn from. Some things came quickly and I acknowledged them, asked for forgiveness, and for the help not to return to them. Other issues and incidents took longer to unearth. I had to be open to the possibility that my own heart had hidden them from my sight and now the truth was being revealed.

During this season of soul searching, God seemed to be growing in me both greater spiritual dependence and authority. While my influence was being diminished at the church, He provided opportunities for me to encounter and influence people outside of our church. What God was teaching me caused the members of our congregation to notice a new depth to my preaching. He was at work transforming me, even if I could not always see or understand it. God was redeeming all of the hardship for good.

Part of what made redemption possible was learning to rest. By rest, I do not mean ceasing activity; what I mean is the ability to trust that God is at work in the current circumstances enough to release control and leave it in His hands. To enter this space, I had to trust that what He was doing would result in good, even if all the evidence in the present moment seemed to indicate otherwise. Developing this capacity involved both knowing His character and the willingness to make choices based upon it.

When You Choose

Intellectually and theologically, I knew God is good. I could visualize the picture painted of Him in Matthew 7:11 as a father who knows how to give good gifts to his children when they ask. I knew this did not mean I would receive everything I asked for, but it did mean I could trust Him to hear me and respond when I cried out. This is much easier to say than it is to believe, especially when the things you are praying for never seem to come to fruition and the very things you fear will take place keep happening.

My heart was tempted to believe He was out to punish or shame me because of my failures, but this is not consistent with who He is or how He has acted toward us. It was in the middle of this tension I had to answer the questions: Would I be willing to give more than intellectual assent to what I understood to be true regarding the character and nature of my heavenly Father? Would I be willing to walk in light of the truth, even though I might not recognize the good of my circumstances in the present moment?

Luke 11 recounts the same instructions Jesus gave us on how to pray in Matthew 7, but there is a slight difference. Instead of the Father in heaven giving "good gifts to those who ask him," as it states in the Matthew passage, Luke tells us the Father in heaven will "give the Holy Spirit to those who ask him." My prayers grew beyond a cry to change my circumstances; they became a cry for the Father to guide me by the Holy Spirit. I needed the Spirit to help me see the truth about what I really believed and how it affected my capacity to enter rest through trust.

I spent forty days away from home as I walked the Camino. Tammie will tell you that during the time I was away she never really rested well. When I am gone, she never feels completely safe, even when our fully-grown children are in the house. Noises she would never notice when I am home suddenly become a cause for alarm. In my absence, she struggles to go to bed at a decent hour because she knows how long the night will feel. It is difficult for her to get a good night's sleep.

When I am home, however, Tammie's anxiety goes away. My presence makes her feel safe and secure. She has no idea what I would do if the house caught on fire or an intruder entered our home, but she has seen me handle enough situations to have confidence I will respond appropriately to whatever circumstance arises. This gives her a sense of security and makes her feel safe enough to rest.

Part of what I had to learn was this same kind of trust in my heavenly Father. He has handled enough situations in my past for me to trust He would respond appropriately to the present. I needed to remind myself of these things. I also needed to begin looking for how He might be at work in the here and now. Being able to identify the ways in which He was meeting me in the present helped bolster my confidence He could be trusted for my future.

There are no easy routes to this kind of trust, but choosing not to walk this path is even harder. Immediately following the passage in Isaiah 30 that calls us to repentance, rest, quietness, and trust are the words, "But you would have none of it." The next few verses give us a picture of what the people of Israel chose instead. They looked to their ability to make a quick getaway on their horses to provide them the salvation and strength God had promised, if only they would trust Him. What would be the consequences of their decision? They would be forced to flee, their pursuers would be swift, and they would be left as a banner on a hill, reminding others what it looks like to refuse to trust and enter the rest God has offered.

> In repentance and rest is your salvation,
>   in quietness and trust is your strength,
>   but you would have none of it.
> You said, 'No, we will flee on horses.'
>   Therefore you will flee!
> You said, 'We will ride off on swift horses.'
>   Therefore your pursuers will be swift!
> A thousand will flee
>   at the threat of one;
> at the threat of five
>   you will all flee away,
> till you are left
>   like a flagstaff on a mountaintop,
>   like a banner on a hill. (Isaiah 30:15-17)

While I was tempted to respond to my circumstances by exercising control and trusting in what I could muster, my deepest desire was not to trust in "horses". I did not want to know the experience of being overcome with fear at the sight of my enemies. I longed for my mind and emotions to be saturated with the truth of who God really is and to be renewed by this knowledge.

For periods of time, I knew what it was to be quiet and experience rest. That did not, however, erase my capacity to return to old patterns. Even after days and weeks of walking in the way that leads to salvation and strength, some new difficulty would emerge at church and my heart would become anxious. My mind would race to find a way to fix and control the situation. After formulating a plan, I

THE GOOD WAY

would be tempted to act on it. The Spirit was gracious enough to protect me from these disordered responses of my heart and remind me through Scripture, prayer, or a friend what God was calling me to. When this happened, all I could do was to return again to the choice presented to me each day—to step onto the path of humility and ask for the Spirit's help to quiet my heart and enter into rest.

Chapter Four

SUSPICIONS

By the time I arrived in Roncevaux, at the end of the first day, I was tired, wet, and sore. The cold had sapped my energy, and it was all I could do to drop my pack on the ground in the hall of the albergue and get out my Pilgrim's Passport to check in. Though exhausted, I was also excited. One of the most difficult days was behind me. I had made it up and over the Pyrenees, and I was about to receive a stamp that would be a lasting testimony to this accomplishment. A smile formed on my tired face as I checked in and presented my passport to the man behind the desk. It took only a few moments for him to write down my information, stamp my passport, and take my Euros.

I had been given a bed on the third floor. Though not excited about climbing all those stairs, I was happy to have arrived and to have a bed. When I walked back into the hall, a man was crouched over my pack, fiddling with something. The online forums I'd read had warned about people who find their way into the albergues and help themselves to the property of unsuspecting pilgrims. This was my first thought when I saw this person bent over my pack, and it must have been apparent in my facial expression and tone of voice when I asked the man if he needed help with something. He immediately began to apologize and explain his actions. He introduced himself as Sergio and pointed out that when I had dropped my pack on the floor, the waist strap and buckle had come to rest in the middle of the hall. He mentioned that the buckle was made of plastic and would break very easily if someone were to step on it. He added, "I was afraid someone might not see it, and so I wanted to move it out of the way."

I could tell he was not sure I was buying his story. I thanked him for his help and concern, even though my suspicion had not totally disappeared. I picked up my pack and began the climb to the third floor. As much as I was focused on getting out of my wet, cold clothes and into a hot shower, I could not shake what had just taken place. I was uncomfortable with the thought that I had jumped so quickly to assume Sergio was up to something. He immediately picked up on my suspicion and quickly tried to explain what was taking place. I had jumped to a conclusion that built an immediate wall between us. This is not how I wanted to walk the Camino. It is not how I want to walk through life. Before I got to my bed, I decided the next time I saw Sergio I was going to reach out to him in warmth and love.

The following day, I saw the Sergio and engaged him in conversation. I acknowledged the awkwardness of our first meeting and tried to put it behind us. I learned that Sergio was from Brazil, taught physical education, loved his wife and family dearly, and was also walking the Camino alone. As I got to know him more over the next few days, I discovered the kindness he showed me in the

Suspicions

hall was a true expression of who he was. He quickly became part of my "Camino family," a fellow traveler with a deepening bond. We ended up walking two-thirds of the way together, spending many nights sharing a meal and talking over a glass of *vino tinto* (red wine).

My first encounter with Sergio forced me to face a harsh reality about myself: I had come to question whether I could trust those around me to care for my well-being or to speak truthfully about their motives. It was a defensiveness born of hurt and what felt like betrayal. This skeptical attitude was now intruding on my experience of community on the Camino. I did not want to walk the Camino mistrustful of the people I was traveling with. This would build barriers between us and affect our ability to learn from one another. I wanted to be open to whatever a person might offer in terms of friendship, wisdom, and love. I wanted to see them as a gift, not a threat.

This way of walking was not unfamiliar to me. It is how I had tried to live as a follower of Christ and a servant of His people. Over the previous two years, however, the number of people who felt safe had greatly diminished. At times, it seemed there were only a handful of trustworthy people left in my world. This perspective led to an increasing sense of loneliness and isolation.

All of this was compounded by a distorted view of what it meant to keep from "scattering the sheep." Over time, the church leadership had developed the perspective that at times it is better to withhold some information from the congregation in order to preserve unity. Because of a history of contentious meetings and a church split, maintaining unity (or at least the appearance of unity) became one of our highest values. We would talk about and celebrate the good things God was doing, but when hard situations arose, we would "protect" the congregation by keeping them as quiet as possible. We kept secrets in order to keep the sheep safe.

What I believe leaders need to understand is that sheep rely heavily on their senses to keep themselves safe. They are adept at recognizing trouble. They are able to perceive a disconnect between what is being shared, and what they see and sense is taking place. I do not believe any leader ever stood up and intentionally lied to the congregation, but as one person said to me after hearing an explanation for a staff member's leaving, "A half truth is not the truth." Providing partial or piecemeal information did not build unity. It did not create an environment of safety and security. In fact, it created an environment where people did not fully trust leadership, raising suspicions about what was really going on behind the scenes.

When I was on the leadership team that made decisions about what would be shared, the effects of this style of communication were hard for me to see, let alone admit. But now having experienced being marginalized, I could see more clearly the seclusion it creates. When the news about Tammie's resignation was conveyed to the congregation, the reasons were not mentioned. Maybe this was appropriate and it would have been fine if it had been left there, but it was not. Leaders offered the perspective that after seventeen years of ministering to children, "Miss Tammie" would once again be able to join the congregation in "Big Church." While this was factually true, it was never her motivation for stepping down.

In truth, Tammie's heart ached because she was not able to be with the children each week. When well-intentioned people told her enthusiastically how wonderful it was that she could finally go to church with the adults, it would cut her to the core. Often, she would have to make a quick exit before tears filled her eyes. She could not talk openly about how much it hurt not to be with the children. She also could not bring herself to affirm the misconception she was excited about the change. She simply had to find ways to avoid the questions and let comments pass. The result was a growing sense of loneliness and isolation.

As hard as this situation was, I fully acknowledge that I was part of this dysfunctional system for many years. I have thought about others who may have experienced and felt what we were now going through. For those who came to mind, I sought them out in order to ask forgiveness and open up a dialogue. Some were willing. For others, the pain was still too great. Because I was there, I know our intent was never to cause hurt, but that does not change the fact we did. For anyone who might be reading this and thinking, *Good, he finally knows what I felt*, I think I do, and I am sorry. Please forgive me.

Within just a few months of Tammie's resignation, the senior pastor had resigned as well. I should have seen it coming. We had gotten together at the beginning of summer to talk about the teaching series for the fall and winter. Each time we had this kind of meeting I would always suggest we teach through the book of Galatians. The senior pastor would always protest and give some reason why he did not want to preach through the book. It had almost become a game between us. I would come up with my best reasons for choosing the book and he would have his best rational for saying no. In this meeting I suggested Galatians once again. This time, he said we ought to teach it in January. I was so surprised and thrilled by his consent, the thought never crossed my mind he might be willing to put it on the calendar because he knew he would not be there.

In early September, I received an email from a friend outside the church asking me if our pastor had stepped down. I did not know how he had heard about it or if it was even true. I sat down with the senior pastor to let him know about the email and asked him if it were true. It was. Not long after our meeting, a letter went out to the congregation informing them of his resignation and reasons for leaving. In his letter, he told the congregation he recognized it was time to move on because when it came to leading the church, he had lost his voice. What he shared was the truth.

Almost immediately you could see the relief in him. He set aside our planned teaching series and spent the last four weeks preaching on things close to his heart. It was powerful. On the first weekend in November, at our church's annual celebration, we celebrated his ministry and said goodbye. It was an appropriate commemoration of his service and impact. I think he felt honored.

I had always known when the senior pastor left there was a good chance I would be gone as well. We had worked in partnership for so long, I knew it would be hard for a new senior pastor to come into the church and keep the executive pastor from the prior administration. I wondered if God had moved me out of that position to protect me. I also knew the forces which had been at work in the past year were still present. There was no chance of an elder board that had been convinced to remove me from my position would consider me as a candidate for senior pastor. Despite the encouragement from many in the congregation, I chose not to apply.

Suspicions

We had lost three significant staff members in the previous few months—four in the last year. Our church was reeling from all of the loss and transition. My role, best as I could discern it, was to bring whatever stability I could until the new senior pastor was selected. What happened thereafter was anyone's guess.

As a church, we went from November through Easter without much drop in attendance. Giving was lagging a bit, but we had seen worse. People seemed to be sticking with the church until the new pastor came. Then came a Monday morning, when I had just come out of a meeting with one of my fellow staff members. I had told him how well I thought his teaching had gone the previous Sunday and asked for input on the message I was preparing for the next Sunday. He ended our time by asking if he could pray for me. It was a gracious prayer on my behalf. I was touched, in part because we had known each other for a long time and there had been rough times in our past. I remember thinking as I walked out of his office, *Lord, if my time at this church is coming to an end, thank you for the gift of seeing this relationship come full circle.*

Back in my office, I pulled out my computer and Bible to begin outlining my sermon. A half-hour later, the executive pastor (my replacement) knocked on my door. He said the elder chairman wanted to see me in the pastor's office. I followed him down the hall to the office. The elder chairman got right to the point and told me that because of the current financial position of the church, the elders had decided to lay off two staff members. I was one of them. It was not totally unexpected, but it still was a surprise. After explaining their position and my severance package, I was informed I needed to have my office cleared out by Wednesday. After 21 years of service, I was given 48 hours to vacate my office. I asked when they had planned for me to say goodbye to the congregation. The elder chairman said they had not given it any thought and turned to the executive pastor. He indicated they were not planning on doing very much to mark my transition. This would be a departure from how we had handled these kinds of transitions in the past.

I then asked them what would become of my daughter's involvement on the summer missions trip on which she was a team member. They had not thought about this either. The executive pastor said they would still want her to go if she desired to do so. My daughter was getting ready to graduate high school and the high school group at the church. Another two months and this transition would have had such a different impact on my family, but it did not appear that much thought had gone into the decision.

With the help of a friend, I cleared my office out that night. I had occupied the space for twenty-one years. In less than two hours, it was empty. Tammie had come to the church to sit and pray in the sanctuary one last time while we packed up. It was the place where we had stood to be married, dedicated our children, ministered, and shared life with people. After that night, it would never be the same. Tuesday morning, I attended my last staff meeting, along with the other pastor who was being laid off. With the news of our layoffs communicated, the rest of the meeting provided time for people to speak words of encouragement to us. On Wednesday, I returned to the office to sign my separation papers and receive my final check.

It was finished.

Believe it or not, as hard as this season was, I have

Suspicions

come to see much of it as good. For months afterward, Tammie and I would share our story with our mentors or counselors outside of our church, and a look of shock would come across their faces. The intensity of their reaction would sometimes surprise us, but it also helped us understand just how broken and damaging much of the process had been. When you grow up in a dysfunctional home, even if it is a ministry home, you often cannot clearly see how it has impacted you. The reaction of others to our story helped us to recognize how numb we were to what the environment had become. It would take time, and being a part of other bodies of believers, before we could fully comprehend the brokenness.

While the experience was painful, it has not caused me to give up hope in the church. I believe it is possible for the Kingdom of God to be alive and active in a community of His followers. I also have come to believe you cannot become that kind of community by any means which is not consistent with the values of the Kingdom and the person of Christ. Where inconsistencies reveal themselves, the move is not to ignore or hide them. We must be willing to acknowledge them, turn from them and step more fully into the way of Jesus. Since no church or leader is perfect, we will all come to these places. I have, and the experience has changed me as a leader. There are ways I have led in the past that will not be part of my future ministry because of what I have come to know and understand in this past season.

The other positive change came in how much of my identity I find in my place of ministry. Much of my heart had become attached to the people and place where I had served. In many ways, my identity and significance were tied up in them. Some of this was healthy and normal. We are in many ways defined by the community to which we belong. I love the people of that church, and I enjoyed using my gifts to serve them. I was willing to invest my whole life in building an environment where together we could learn to live and love like Jesus.

On the other hand, my identity could not be rooted in the people I ministered to or the place I served. Our identity as Christ followers can only be found in Him. Theologically I knew this was true, but experientially I looked to other sources to define who I was. Being torn from the people and place I served was an opportunity to root my soul in the vastness of Christ's love and the identity bestowed upon me through Him. It was also a chance to allow the Spirit to prune from my life anything I might be tempted to substitute for my identity in Christ.

This is a painful process and often requires letting go of significant things. It is also the birthplace of great freedom. It is powerful and life giving to learn to walk in the reality of your identity in Christ and His love. One of the terms used by early Christian writers to describe this ability is "Indifference." When you think of the word *indifference*, you probably think of *apathy* or *unconcern*. Because of this, Tammie doesn't like it when I use this word in a spiritual context. Instead, she likes to think of the concept as "Regardless." What would it be like to be so rooted in the reality of your identity in Christ that you could love *regardless* of how others treat you? If they are callous and unkind, you have the capacity to respond in love, because you walk in the truth of being fully loved by Jesus Christ. If people lavish love and kindness upon you, your response to them does not change because your love is not conditional—it is grounded in the love you have received from the Father.

Suspicions

This kind of love enables us to love our neighbor as ourselves. It gives us the capacity to forgive those who hurt us. It empowers us to bless those who curse us. It enables us to love our enemies. It does not seek its own, but seeks to benefit others. It does not demand to be served, but finds ways to serve. With this kind of love, you are not enslaved by how others respond to you. It grants you the ability to walk in complete freedom.

You may have heard the phrase, "Hurt people hurt people." I do not believe what took place in my church was born out of malice. If somehow I could trace each hurtful action back to its origin, I think I would discover each was born out of some hidden fear or wound. People who are wounded and broken will end up wounding and breaking others unless the cycle is interrupted. My story may be different from yours, but undoubtedly you have been hurt in some way. Each one of us can point to wounds caused by someone else's wounds. Having been caught in the collateral damage, however, does not mean we have to pass it on.

There is another phrase: "Free people free people." Despite having experienced great hurt, I do not desire to pass along the pain. I do not wish hurt on those who hurt me. Jesus provided us with a healing path to follow. He said, "If the Son makes you free, you will be free indeed" (John 8:36). Jesus came to set us free from sin, death, and unrighteousness. He came to offer the gifts of forgiveness, life, and freedom. When we hurt, we have a choice: Will we take the pain we have received and pass it on to someone else, or will we recognize the only way to heal the pain is to walk in the freedom found in Christ?

After returning home from the Camino, I received an email inviting Tammie and I to a potluck for a friend connected with the church where we had served. When I looked at the list of people who had received an invitation, I had mixed emotions. Some were people I have missed; I was excited by the possibility of sharing a meal with them. There were also people on that list who were at the center of the hurt we experienced. Six or eight months prior, their names would have been enough for me to simply hit the delete button. I would have been allowing my hurt to control my decisions. That's not the way I want to live.

Rather than deleting the message, I signed us up for a side dish and told Tammie we were going. We had no idea how awkward the dinner might be. I had no control over how those who hurt us would feel or respond to our presence. In truth, I did not even have control over how I would feel when I walked through the door. I could, however, choose to walk in light of my identity in Christ. I could allow His love, not my hurt, to determine my ability to love regardless. Walking like this is true freedom. It is also an invitation for others to break out of the cycle of hurt and be free. Instead of being one who spreads pain, it is possible to become an instrument of healing. This is how Christ walked. I desire to follow in His footsteps. It is a significant part of what it means to walk in the good way.

Chapter Five

BEING WITH

My interaction with Sergio was not the first opportunity I had to choose how I would walk in relationship to others. Days before, I met another pilgrim who would cause me to ponder how I would relate to the people I would meet. I had been traveling for fifteen hours by the time I arrived at Charles de Gaulle Airport in Paris. I did not sleep on the red-eye flight to Europe. This did not change my decision to stay up all day in order to get acclimated to the local time as quickly as possible. In three hours, my train to Bayonne would depart from the station located at the airport. I consumed copious amounts of coffee and then found a bench, perched on a platform, overlooking the tracks. Though located outdoors, it was protected from the elements. Perfect—comfortable enough to stretch out on, but cold enough to keep me from dozing off.

Not long after I settled into my spot, a woman approached me and asked if I was planning to walk the Camino. Apparently, my backpack and the walking poles tied to it gave me away. I told her I was, and given the number of North Face logos on her clothing, I had a feeling she would be walking as well. So I said, "You, too?" She said yes and explained that she had walked it last fall. She mentioned her difficulty with tendonitis at first, but overall it was a wonderful experience.

Not wanting to miss the opportunity to learn from someone who had been there, I asked, "What do you wish you would have known before you started last time and what are you doing differently this time?" Her main advice was to take it slow in the beginning. She did not her first time out, and she believed it contributed to her injury. We talked about our reasons for walking and expectations we were bringing to the Camino. We also discovered we would be on the same train to Bayonne. While I was stopping there for the night, she would continue on to St. Jean when we arrived.

Soon, she meandered back over to the bench where she had left her luggage. A few minutes later, she came back with a piece of paper she had torn out of a notepad. On it she had written some things worth seeing and parts of the Camino where she had wished she had taken alternative routes. I thanked her and tucked the piece of paper away in my journal for future reference. Then she warned me along the way I would encounter what she called the "walking wounded." These were people who had come to the Camino to process a significant hurt or loss. She told me a story of a woman she had walked with in the fall who kept talking as if her dead husband was walking with them. She would say things like, "Frank is right behind us." It took my new acquaintance several days to realize that indeed Frank was walking right behind them—her friend was carrying his ashes in her pack.

At first, it seemed she brought up this story as an invitation to enter into the pain of others. But as I listened to her throughout the day, I came to realize the walking wounded seemed to be more of an irritation to her than an opportunity for compassion. While we did not ride in the same car on the train, we would bump into each other at the stops where we had to wait for our connecting trains. These interactions allowed me to piece together her story. It seems she had gone through her own season of loss and hurt. I could not help but wonder if her annoyance with the walking wounded stemmed from her own deep wounds. There is nothing more detrimental to our attempts to deny what is going on internally than to see it embodied in someone standing right in front of us. I wondered if I would be an irritation to her if she could see the wounds I was carrying. I hoped not, but I hadn't come all this way to walk in anything but the truth of who I was and what I had experienced. In fact, I wanted my own commitment to authenticity to encourage the same in others I encountered.

If you are going to journey with the walking wounded, the first thing you have to do is set aside your desire to *fix*. Several months before I left for the Camino, I heard a speaker talk about the way in which we live in community with one another. In particular, she was talking to Christian leaders and the posture we take with the people we serve. There are three ways in which we can relate to others: we can do things *for* someone; we can do things *to* someone; or we can do things *with* someone. If we are honest with ourselves, most of us prefer the *for* and the *to* approaches. We like to do things *for* people because it gives us a sense of being benevolent—and makes us feel valuable and necessary. We also like to do things *to* people because it allows us to feel in control of the circumstances and assert our will onto others. Sometimes it may be necessary to do things *for* and *to* others, but we have to be careful since these strategies tend to lead to dependence, not community.

To do things *with* others is far different. We are not setting ourselves above them or encouraging them to become reliant on us—we are walking with them. We are not controlling and defining their experience—we are sharing it. Having an attitude of *with* enables us to feel known, accepted, and loved. In *with*, we are not alone or isolated, but discover true community. *With* has the capacity to allow us to be completely honest with ourselves, others, and God. *With* allows the other to heal. In the process, we do a fair bit of healing ourselves.

Later, on the Camino, I was walking with a woman who asked me advice on how she could help a friend of hers. The friend had experienced significant hurt and loss in the recent past and struggled to move beyond it. The women I was talking with felt frustrated at not being able to help her friend get past it. She asked for my input. What she was really asking was a *for* or a *to* question: "What do I do for or to my friend to make the situation better?" I told her I was pretty sure there was not anything she could do to "fix" her friend.

"Heck," I added, "we cannot even fix ourselves. But what you might be able to offer is the gift of simply being *with* your friend. This is much harder. It involves listening and maybe asking questions that help bring clarity to what your friend is thinking and feeling. It may mean listening to the same story several times, but in the process you will help your friend feel loved and accepted. It means resisting the urge to give advice. Your friend may even ask you to tell her what to do. Don't fall into that trap. The most powerful thing you can do is just be with her."

Being With

The Camino lends itself to living like this with people. It calls out our capacity of being with others: physically, intellectually, emotionally, spiritually, and socially. Each one of these aspects plays a part in making us human and reflecting in us the image of God. Each aspect has also been damaged and malformed by sin and its effects. We often try to hide the damage with the stuff that fills our lives. How much of what we spend our money, time, and energy on is designed to somehow numb us to the reality of our brokenness? The Camino strips people of these defenses, whether they are ready for it or not.

Early on, you will find tables in the albergues where pilgrims have deposited items that seemed important to bring along before leaving home and now are no longer deemed significant enough to carry any farther. The pain of lugging a heavy pack over the Pyrenees causes a sudden urge to purge all unnecessary weight. Many have seen the tables full of discarded items as a metaphor for the Camino. As you make the journey, you lay aside the burdens you brought with you. You are walking out from under the weight of the hurt, loss, and unmet expectations that you carried. As you share this experience with others you discover the healing which is possible.

I witnessed a tangible physical expression of this as my Camino family journeyed from Bercianos del real Camino to Mansilla de las Mulas. My friend Helen experienced pain in her knees and struggled as she walked. She was a trouper and pressed on. Just after we passed Reliegos, there was a long flat stretch leading into Mansilla. By the time we all reached this spot it seemed the Camino had turned into a superhighway for pilgrims. Our group, and several others, converged and walked the last five kilometers together. With lots of banter and laughter, the end-of-day stretch goes more smoothly. Helen noticed a man by the name of Rolando. He was quite easy to spot because he would walk past us at a quick pace, but as soon as he got ahead of us, he would stop to sit and rest. It took only a couple of cycles of this before Helen began to wonder if he might be suffering from a similar injury as she was. The next time she came to him, she asked if he was also suffering knee pain.

Rolando replied that his knees felt fine. It was his pack that was killing him. Before beginning the Camino, he had camped along the way in France. He did not know if there would be opportunity to camp along the Camino so he kept all his gear and now carried it with him. Helen's kind words and willingness to listen to Rolando's struggle must have been enough to make him forget the weight for a time because he walked with us the rest of the way into Mansilla. The next day he kept commenting on how heavy his pack was. Many suggested he consider mailing ahead anything he would not need on the journey. When we reached Leon, Rolando finally removed all unnecessary items from his pack and mailed them to Santiago. When he returned from the post office, he announced he had lightened his load by nine kilograms (nearly twenty pounds). To put this in perspective, my backpack and everything in it weighed only nine kilograms. It was as if Rolando had been carrying his pack and mine the entire way.

I imagine Helen could have tried to hide her knee discomfort. After all, would it not be better to be seen as strong and invincible rather than weak and ailing, even if it was not true? So many of us walk through life trying to convince others—and even ourselves—that we are not as wounded as we really are. Pride had no such control over

Helen. Instead, she was willing to be open and honest with a complete stranger about her struggles; in turn, he was invited to be open and honest about his. Eventually, this connection changed everything. Rolando no longer walked alone. While the source of his discomfort was not the same as Helen's, somehow sharing their burdens made it easier for Helen to walk. She was given strength to press on. In the days to come, Helen's knees would feel much better and Rolando's pack would be much lighter. In some ways you could say each of them was able to find healing—healing fostered in part by their willingness to be with one another. By the end of the journey, they had shared intellectually, emotionally, spiritually, and socially as much as they shared physically on the first day. The impact reached beyond Helen and Rolando. It affected our entire Camino family as Rolando was grafted in and as we also shared in being with one another.

While I had my fair share of physical pain on the Camino, the hurt I brought with me was the pain of being cleaved from a community that was so much a part of me; it was hard to think of myself as separate from it. When the Bible speaks of the church, it does not talk about business models or organizational structures. It uses the image of a family, with references to brothers and sisters, adopted children, and joint heirs with Christ. The people I served with were not fellow employees; the people we served were not "clients" or "constituents." They were all family. What I had experienced felt like a shunning rather than the loving embrace of family. This caused hurt and great loss. To be honest, it left me wondering if it was even possible to enter back into community without first erecting protective walls.

Scripture also speaks of the church as a body. Like the

human body, its parts are dependent upon one another for health and welfare. As 1 Corinthians 12:21 points out, it would be ridiculous for the eye to say to the hand, "I don't need you." It seemed just as peculiar for me to imagine myself being part of any other community than the one I was separated from. I guess I could pretend it did not hurt as much as it did, but it would have been as silly as Helen acting as if her knees were fine. What would have been lost if she had pretended and not reached out to Rolando? What would be lost in my life if I chose to pretend the pain was not there? Unfortunately, that is exactly how many of us feel we must live in order to protect ourselves.

A friend stopped by recently to check in on me and hear about my trip. She had also been to a foreign country and spent significant time with people she'd just met. After we each had shared a few of our stories, Tammie asked our friend what touched her heart the most on the trip. Instantly, her eyes filled with tears and she told of being fully accepted into the community she was visiting. She talked about what it was like to feel accepted exactly as she was by people she barely knew. The experience struck a deep chord in her heart.

Unfortunately, having others allow her to be herself is not something she regularly encounters at home. Tammie's eyes filled with tears as well and mentioned that the smallest act of compassion during our transition caused her to well up. We are so accustomed to having people try to do something *for* and *to* us that the floodgates of our hearts open when someone simply chooses to be *with* us. The deluge helps to cleanse our hearts and promote healing.

Three days before the end of the Camino, it rained. It was light at first, which made me wonder if I needed to don my poncho. Soon, the rain progressed from light to moderate to hard, and I had no choice but to put on my rain cover. This part of the trail was not nearly as steep as the first few days, so the rain was not nearly as unwelcomed. A month earlier, the rain seemed to be working against us, trying to keep us from navigating the Pyrenees. It felt like a mean rain. Now, the precipitation seemed much kinder. It still came down hard, but now it felt like a gift rather than a curse.

As we walked on, I noticed how the rain washed the dust from the trail, something I was much more aware of after walking through the Meseta. There, it might have made a muddy quagmire; here, the rain released the scent of the eucalyptus trees in the forest around us. It smelled wonderful. By midday, our raingear had been stored and the sun peeked out. The green, leafy forest was freshly washed and vibrant. The streams of light illumined the mist that was formed by the sun's heat evaporating puddles. It was as if the earlier rain earlier had cleansed the land and prepared it to display what we now could enjoy as we made our way along its paths and trails.

The same thing happens when we experience being *with*. It helps to cleanse the human heart, making it possible to display the glory that can only be revealed as hurt is washed away.

Chapter Six

WAITING

The walk from Roncevaux to Zubiri was almost entirely downhill. Reason would tell you that descending would be much easier, but for me it was not. The heavy rains of the previous day had made the trail slippery and unstable. If the knee-pounding descent was not enough, you now had to be extra careful that your feet did not slide out from under you, depositing you on your behind or, worse, sending you tumbling headfirst. My spill on the first day made me well aware of the possibility.

Now, I walked gingerly as I made my way along the path. This did not keep me from slipping and sliding from time to time. The sudden feeling that I was about to do the splits or go airborne caused me to tense up and move stiffly. While the muscles which ached as I climbed the mountains on the first day were allowed to rest, different joints and muscles now cried out in pain.

By the time I walked into Zubiri, I was ready to be done for the day. The guidebook suggested we walk another five kilometers, but when I entered the town square I noticed several familiar faces, including Yavidan, one of the people I had met at the albergue in St. Jean. We had also looked out for one another in Roncevaux. She had already taken a look around the small town and found the albergue. She said she was stopping for the day, and my aching feet and knees convinced me it was a good decision to join her. Waiting for the albergue to open, I settled against a wall in the town square. I released my feet from the confines of my shoes, which were still wet from yesterday's slog. Yavidan left her backpack with me and went to explore the streets surrounding the square. It seemed like she had just disappeared from sight when she came running back. The albergue had opened early, and she wanted to check in. I quickly picked up the gear I had stripped off while sitting there and followed her to our home for the night.

The municipal albergue was simple—several large rooms with rows of metal bunk beds. While in Roncevaux, we had stayed in the new wing on a floor where there were no bunk beds. Rather than beds, it felt like we were staying in pods. They were new and comfortable. Each had its own electrical outlet, light, and cabinet for locking up your gear. Now, staring into the Zubiri albergue, Roncevaux seemed like a four-star hotel.

The bathrooms and showers were in a detached building. It was separated from the sleeping areas by a side yard that had several picnic benches and a long clothesline. Attached to the bathrooms was a small kitchen and eating area. We made quick work of selecting our beds, settling our gear and finding the showers. Each albergue is different. In the nicer albergues, the facilities for men and women are separated. In some, men and women share the bathrooms, with single-stall showers where you shower side-by-side. This one featured a common area for sinks and group showers much like you

Waiting

might have had in junior high school. I guess I was going to get to know people, or at least the men on the Camino, much more intimately than I had anticipated.

After a shower, I washed my clothes. Once they were clean and hung on the line to dry, we could get something to eat. It was moving toward midafternoon. I found Yavidan at the corner restaurant, and she invited me to join her. While I probably knew her better than anyone else on the Camino, we still were just getting acquainted. We spent the afternoon sharing why we were walking the Camino and what we had discovered over the first two days. I told her about my family and she told me about hers. We talked about faith, hopes, and dreams. I remember thinking, *If my days on the Camino are going to be filled with these kinds of conversations, it will be a very rich time.*

After lunch we headed back to the albergue and planted ourselves on the picnic benches in the yard. This was a wonderful way to make new friends. Brant and Litsa had shown up, and we got to know them better. For the first time we met Jeff and Karen, followed by others who would came to sit and chat for a while. By late afternoon, some of us decided to head back to the restaurant for a glass of wine.

Because we were still fairly new to the Camino, we introduced ourselves around the table and shared a bit of our story. This would be the only time I spent with some of these people; others I would end up walking with for days or weeks. It was here I would first meet Samantha, Alice, Junyoung, and Emily. These people, as well as others I had yet to meet, would weave their lives into the fabric of my journey in both big and small ways. I did not realize it fully in the moment, but together we were beginning to establish a rhythm that would allow us to share much more than a drink before dinner and our experience of the day.

For me, that rhythm did not yet include walking with others. I would rise early in the morning, and I was usually one of the first to leave the albergue, starting to walk just as the sun rose. Before the Camino, I had been excited about new relationships, but that was not my primary reason for walking. I had anticipated this would be a physical expression of the internal-spiritual journey I had been traveling for almost two years. One of the most significant aspects of this season had been learning to wait. Early on, God had impressed upon me Psalm 27:14: "Wait for the Lord; be strong and take heart and wait for the Lord." While I had hoped the transition time would be short, by the time I set out on the Camino it had been nearly thirteen months since I had left the church.

Each morning as I began to walk, I anticipated that God would speak clearly to me about what was next for my life. I didn't begin my day early because I did not wish to be with others, but because I wanted to hear from God. Psalm 27:13 says, "I remain confident of this: I will see the goodness of the Lord in the land of the living." I expected the Lord to reveal His goodness to me. My heart was attuned, eager to hear His voice.

In the beginning, I never predicted I would be in such a long waiting period. Within a month of being laid off, I interviewed via Skype with a church in the Pacific Northwest. The interview went well and by the time session ended, I felt a fondness for the people who made up the search team. Tammie and I happened to be visiting friends in the Seattle area, and the church was just a few hours away. We decided to drive over and check it out.

Waiting

Because of how positive we felt about the interview, we set out that morning with the feeling we might see our new home for the first time. It was exciting.

I cannot fully explain why, but as we got closer to the town where the church was located, I had strong feelings of desolation wash over me. Tammie sat beside me as we drove, unaware of what I was experiencing or the conversation I was having with God. I told Him it felt as if he was stripping everything from us. Was this His intent? Before even arriving at the town, I felt to move here would be full surrender. I was willing, but I wanted to know for sure because it felt as if it would demand so much. We toured the town, drove by the church, and stopped by the visitor's center for information. The woman who worked there fit the job perfectly—she had nothing but praises for the area and the quality of life it offered. She pointed out on a map some excellent places to live, and we headed off to explore her recommendations.

After several hours of exploration, we headed back toward Seattle. As we drove out of town, I asked Tammie what she thought. Up till now, I hadn't told her what I had been feeling. The first words out of her mouth were, "It felt like desolation to me. I think I would cry every day if I lived there."

Moving there would have required us to leave everything we had known. Despite how we felt, we were not yet ready to close the door. We knew we were still reeling from being cut off from the only community we had known for the past Twenty-nine years, and we understood our judgment might be colored by pain. When we returned home, we separately sat down with people who had been offering us counsel.

After talking to our friends and mentors about the

opportunity and what we had experienced when visiting the town, Tammie and I were surprised when we came back to compare notes. What they had each shared with us was similar. In short, they said it is too soon. As one man offered, "You spent thirty years living life with the people of the church. You have not yet been able to let go of them. There is no space for you to embrace a new community, because you have not yet grieved the loss of the last one." We knew that he and the others had spoken the truth. We were not ready to move on. We needed to wait.

One of the reasons people do not like to wait is because it feels like *doing nothing*. Our mental picture of waiting often derives from standing in long lines at Disneyland, sitting at the DMV, or queuing up at the grocery store. We know the waiting leads to something, even something good, but it seems like such a waste of time. During our waiting period, there were times when this is exactly what it felt like. I felt like a player who had been benched. I was now watching others play, anticipating the moment when the coach would put me back in the game. Sitting there felt like such a waste. I was left wondering, how long it would take for the coach to call my number? If I didn't get into this game, would there be another? When would I know?

These are the wrong questions to ask and the wrong posture to take. The kind of waiting Tammie and I were being asked to engage in involved much more than sitting idly on the bench, waiting for our number to be called. At the end of Psalm 33, we are told, "We wait in hope for the Lord; he is our help and our shield. In him our hearts rejoice, for we trust in his holy name. May your unfailing love be with us, Lord, even as we put our hope in you" (vv. 20-22). We can wait in hope because God is our help and protection. The emotional state of the writer goes

Waiting

beyond hope: He had the capacity to rejoice, because of the trust he had in the name of God. In biblical times, a name was more than a way to identify someone; it represented a person's character and nature. The psalmist could trust because he knew the character of God. Knowing who God is and the power He has enabled the psalmist to keep from despairing at his circumstance. Tammie and I were being invited to learn this same kind of hope and trust.

The stanza just before this passage reads:

> No king is saved by the size of his army;
> no warrior escapes by his great strength.
> A horse is a vain hope for deliverance;
> despite all its great strength it cannot save.
> But the eyes of the Lord are on those who fear him,
> on those whose hope is in his unfailing love,
> to deliver them from death
> and keep them alive in famine.
> (Psalm 33:16-19)

I had no plans to raise an army, but how quickly I could be tempted to look to my own strength for deliverance. Immediately after being laid off, I felt the strong urge to move quickly to the next thing. A mentor told me I should do just the opposite. In his experience, pastors who had been in the same place for a long time need six months at least, often a year, before they are ready to move to the next place. I had a hard time accepting this. I did not envision myself out of ministry for three months, let alone a year.

Financially it did not seem like an option either. The church leaders said the fiscal situation that prompted my layoff also prevented them from being able to provide the standard severance package pastors had been given in the past. The sting of this reality was compounded by the fact that the church had decided decades ago to opt out of unemployment and state disability. Many churches and nonprofits do so in order to save money, so the typical safety nets most workers count on were not available.

Thankfully, my good friend Dana offered me a temporary position. His company was installing a new phone system in twenty-four of their warehouses across the United States. By taking the job, I would be able to earn enough to get us through to the end of the year, and Dana's company would save quite a bit on what they would pay if they had a service provider install the systems.

Dana and I had already planned a road trip for June to Oklahoma to visit his mother. There were two warehouses along the way, and we stopped in each location so he could train me. The installation was not too difficult once you understood how the system connected to the existing network. Midway through our first install, I remember thinking, *What am I doing here?* I could do the work, but this was not what I felt called to do. Long before I had heard the phrase "If you do not humble yourself to the Camino, the Camino will humble you," I was being given the opportunity to choose humility. I was actually kneeling at the desk of one of the salespersons, running wires from his computer to the phone, when I turned to the Lord in my heart and said, *I am willing to be a servant here, if this is what you have for me.*

The job was slated to take only two months. I would need to travel five days a week and return home on weekends. As far as the installation process went, it was not difficult to comprehend but did require considerable

Waiting

focus and attention. So there was no way I could dwell on my difficult circumstances while installing phones. This was a much bigger gift than I would have imagined it to be in the beginning. Like an injury that needs rest to heal, my heart desperately needed rest from the past year and a half of transition and loss. This job provided my heart the space it needed to heal. One of my mentors called it a working sabbatical.

I would arrive first thing in the morning at a location and spend most of the day installing the infrastructure for the new phone network and prepare to switch systems. We could not make this change until the office was closed and the phones turned off for the evening. Normally someone from the office would have to stay with me until the switchover was complete and the old phone system was removed. After several installs, we had this process down pat, but in the beginning it could take up to three hours. This time usually gave me an opportunity to strike up a conversation with the person who stayed.

At one of the locations, we were completing the switchover on a Saturday afternoon. For the person who was forced to work his Saturday, it multiplied the desire to be done quickly. Of course, it turned out to be anything but quick. I could tell he was getting a frustrated, but off site networking issues were taking time to get worked out. While we waited, I asked what he had planned for the rest of the day. He told me he was divorced and his daughter was in town to spend a few weeks with him. He expressed concern about how it would go. She was at that awkward teenage stage where everything a parent does seems wrong, plus the hurt caused by the divorce had caused strain.

I told him my own daughter had just graduated high

school, and I shared what wisdom I could from my own experience of raising a teenager. I also told him I was from a divorced home and did not want to be around my father when I was in high school, but his faithfulness over the years provided a foundation for the relationship we now share. In high school, I said, I would have never imagined we would have the kind of relationship we have as adults. I encouraged him to continue to press in even if it feels like she is pushing him away. Though it would be painful at times, I told him, the effort would be well worth it in the long run. He thanked me for what I had shared.

The fellow must have wondered how a phone installer could feel the freedom to speak from the heart this way, since he asked me, "How long have you been installing phones?" This was my favorite question. I would get asked this question at every other location, usually after a conversation similar to the one I had with this gentleman. Often, I would have guys ask me things like, "Can you remove the porn blocker off my computer?" They would tell me about their drinking and sexual escapades from the night before, or they would sprinkle a generous amount of F-bombs in their conversation. When I told them I recently took this job after twenty-one years as a pastor, their eyes would suddenly open wide. I could almost see them mentally replaying every conversation we'd had over the past twelve hours.

I told this guy the same thing I told the rest of them. For some people, this revelation shut down any future conversation, but for others I could tell it caused them to rethink what they thought of pastors, and we continued to talk. Even on a working sabbatical, God was giving me opportunities to pastor people and show the love, acceptance, and forgiveness of Christ.

Waiting

By the time the two months were over, I felt ready to move on. I thought, *God is good! He gave me the space to heal, and He provided enough income to get through the rest of the year.* Now I was betting He was ready to bring me to the next place of ministry. I was confident by January I would be moving into what was to come next.

In October, a couple of potential opportunities appeared on the horizon. Some I had sought out, others had been unsolicited. Tammie and I decided to go away for a few days to pray and listen for God's leading. We continued to invite others into the process and gave them a synopsis of the prospects before us. Rather than bringing greater clarity, every day we were gone we received another call or email with another opportunity. What we heard most clearly was the word *wait*. This was confirmed by those who were praying on our behalf. Their response could be summed up by one friend who said she heard God say, "Wait, your next position is not ready yet."

Returning home, each of the opportunities went away, either because we told them no or because the churches decided to go in a different direction. We were not discouraged. We felt like we had asked God for direction, and we were confident he had told us to wait. We came to believe that the *Yes* would be determined by the *Nos*. Each closed door would take us a step closer to one that would open for us. Since there were so many closed doors in a short span, I hoped it meant our open door would appear soon.

Waiting is much easier when you have the opportunity to earn enough to pay the bills. Come January, the money I had earned was all spent. We had savings to live on, but there is something significantly different about earning enough to meet your needs and watching your savings dwindle each month. Waiting was taking on a whole new meaning. Rather than feeling like we were getting closer to the open door, I had the distinct feeling we were walking down a long corridor. This process could take far longer than we had hoped and believed. We were learning to trust God's character and capacity to help in a new way and, frankly, it was uncomfortable.

My discomfort increased because of the responses I would get when I bumped into people from my old church. Like me, they expected I would have moved into a new place of ministry by now. When they asked what I was doing, I would answer, "I'm teaching a class as an adjunct professor and meeting with a few people for spiritual direction, but mostly I am waiting for God to lead me to my next place." They would try to encourage me by saying they knew God had something for me and He would reveal it soon. Often, there was no congruence between what they said and what I could see in their body language. Even though hopeful words were coming out of their mouth, the look on their face revealed how unsettled my circumstance made them feel. It would have been easier for all of us if I had a new position.

These interactions compounded my own sense of being unsettled. I wanted to wait on the Lord with the same hope and trust as the psalmist. In the midst of the waiting, I wanted to have a heart that rejoiced. Each of these conversations would force me to choose again between depending on my own strength and trusting God. Like Peter responded when asked by Jesus if he wanted to head in a different direction, I would find myself crying out to God, "Lord, to whom shall *I* go? You have the words of eternal life" (John 6:68). Knowing there is no other place to find life, I had no choice but to wait.

Waiting

* * *

Each morning I awoke on the Camino and began to walk was an exercise in continuing to learn to wait in hope. I was being taught to trust in God's ability to help and save, knowing His character never changes. I could not control when He would choose to move or speak. All I could do was to recommit each new day to actively waiting on Him. I was learning to walk farther and farther through a dark corridor, still believing that the source of light could be trusted.

Chapter Seven

BECOMING FAMILY

I cannot say exactly when it happened. I know it took place somewhere between sitting around the table in Zubiri and our stop for a café con leche in Los Arcos. We had made the transition from acquaintances who happened to be walking in the same direction to a community centered on a common purpose and finally to a family. We had arrived in Los Arcos around noon. We found a café-bar in the middle of town where we could get something to drink and decided together what was next.

Normally, when we came to the town where we planned to stop, we immediately made our way to the albergue, but not today. The walk from Estella had been a relatively short one, only 21.1 kilometers. Tomorrow was scheduled to be a bit longer, 28.6 kilometers. We were feeling good, the day was beautiful, and it was only eight more kilometers to Torres del Rio. We spent some time deliberating over the pros and cons of going on. Only after we called ahead to make sure we would have a place to stay did we make the decision to move on. Sergio had made it to Los Arcos and found us in the square. It was always a joy to see him. We asked him to continue on with

THE GOOD WAY

us, but he was suffering from shin splints and decided to stop for the day. We wished him well, promised to look for him in Logrono, and then set out for our afternoon of walking.

We traveled on a broad, level dirt road that cut its way through vineyards and wheat fields. A kilometer before Torres del Rio stood the village of Sansol. It sat on the only hill between our destination and us and provided a distant marker, allowing us to judge our progress. Those who set out together included Yavidan, Emily, Marta, Ki, Junyoung, and myself. It was our seventh day on the Camino. Eight days ago, we had no idea the others existed. Now, as we walked, I had the distinct feeling we had become a family.

Our walking and talking came easily. Sometimes we would all be together, laughing and singing together. At other times we would spread out in groups of two or three. These groups would shift and morph. We walked under a blue sky that was filled with billowy white clouds and along the tan gravel carpet, which seemed to be rolled out in welcome for us. In the smaller groups, we were able to open our hearts to one another. We discussed life and faith. We explored what it means to be in relationship with others, and they asked me to tell them the secret of being married for twenty-seven years. I was also able to share why I had chosen to follow Christ and what my deepest desire was for this season of life.

To illustrate my longing, I pulled out my iPod and played the song "Oceans" by Hillsong United. The lyrics spoke of being led by the Spirit of God to be able to trust Him without any limitations. They were an invitation for the Spirit to lead where we could not go in our own strength and a declaration of the desire to find our faith grow stronger as we discovered the presence of Christ in that place.

This is the prayer of my heart. While there was no ocean in sight, the dirt road became the water upon which we walked. The path, which seemed to extend out into the distance without end, felt like a place where trust was without borders as I journeyed with people who had the capacity to hold one another's hearts. We walked in silence as the song played. When it ended, Yavidan simply said it was beautiful.

How did we get here? How do you go from being total strangers one day and seven days later feeling as if you are family? It is easier than you think, but it does require a willingness to make it happen. The Camino places you in a posture that enables this kind of community to develop, almost without you knowing it is happening. While I am sure all of us were excited about the potential of meeting new and interesting people, I do not know if any of us imagined we would become part of a family so quickly. By the time we found ourselves walking along the road, moving toward Torres del Rio, I had come to love these people deeply. I also felt loved and accepted by them. What made this possible?

On paper, we were an unlikely group of people. The seven of us represented five different countries: Italy, Korea, Mexico, Brazil, and the United States. We represented three decades of life, with those in their twenties through forties. Seven languages were spoken among us. We were different culturally, ethnically, socially, and religiously. These differences, however, could not erase the reality that we were humans who bore the image of God, despite whatever woundedness and brokenness we brought with us.

THE GOOD WAY

Being made in His image, we were all designed to live in community. We each possessed a longing to be loved, known, empowered and released. We also shared a common purpose in coming to the Camino, not just to get to Santiago, but also to create the space to be able to ask and ponder the bigger questions of life. This created a foundation from which we could enter into relationship with one another. We were prepared to give to and receive from fellow travelers.

The first place this began to express itself was around the dinner table. It started in St. Jean, continued in Zubiri, and matured at nearly every town we stayed in. Some nights it was simply taking in the pilgrim meal at a café-bar. This was a three-course meal with a bottle of wine for eight to ten Euros per person. There were usually five or six starters from which you could choose, an equal number of main dishes, and a few desserts. The food was typically tasty and filling after a long day of walking, but what made the dinners special was the conversation and laughter we shared around the table.

When an albergue had a kitchen, we would choose to cook. This is when it felt like "breaking bread together," as Scripture describes. It would usually begin in the late afternoon when we would decide to make something as a group. Several, if not all of us, would head to the local supermercado or in the smaller towns the tienda (a more limited market). Often, our menu would be determined by what was available. The scarcity of certain foods in some locations forced us to be creative. But be assured, we ate well. The act of shopping was an opportunity for our little family to practice putting others before ourselves and recognizing what each person had to offer for cooking and preparation. I loved the way we were deferential toward one another as we made our selections for the evening.

We all would do our part to prepare the meal. Of course, some of us had more skills than others. I was usually regulated to chopping vegetables, uncorking the wine, setting the table, and washing the dishes. The serious business of cooking the meal had to be left to those who actually possessed abilities in the kitchen. Junyoung explained that part of his purpose on the Camino was to change people's perception of South Korea, and he wanted to help bring this about by cooking good Korean food. Somehow, in the middle of Spain, in villages where there was only a small tienda, he found the ingredients to make some amazing dishes. Ki acted as his sous chef. Marta brought her Italian flare to the table. Yavidan brought skills she learned in Mexico, Italy, and France. Emily, our vegetarian, introduced us to delicious dishes made without meat. Later on the Camino, we would have a Frenchmen make us French toast and a wonderful omelet. People from Germany, New Zealand, Japan, and the USA would all help to make our meals special.

As good as our dinners were, what we ate was not the priority. I remember one meal we shared in Leon. We had gone to the supermercado to buy the ingredients to make wraps. We went to a local park and opened all the food and spread it out on the bags we had carried it in. There was no cooking involved. We did not even have a table. We sat on the ground where we broke our flat bread, shared a bottle of wine, and enjoyed one another's company. What I remember most about this particular meal were the smiles on the faces of the people who shared it.

Our conversations were building upon one another like layers of paint being added to a canvas. What you experience is the depth that has been created by each layer and color. Even if nothing significant was shared at a particular time, the moment was still sweet because of the depth of conversations enjoyed at another meal or while walking. Mealtime allowed us to serve one another and linger in conversation, developing intimacy and connectedness.

Enjoyably, our meals were never exclusive to our little family. In Najera, seven of us set out to make dinner together. As was often the case, we had more than we could possibly eat. By the time we sat down, we had added two more plates, and by the time we got up to wash the dishes, another had joined us. There was always a sense of welcome and sharing at the table. While small groups had shopped for and prepared their own meals, they were always willing to share, whether a sample or a whole plate. If you come from a culture where it almost seems impolite to accept the invitation, it takes some time to get used to saying thank you, rather than no thank you, when someone invites you to join them. Luckily, it only takes one or two experiences of this kind of hospitality to know how loved it can make you feel. Soon, there is no hesitation to join in.

Food was not the only thing people shared. You carry very little on your back on the Camino, and it is impossible to carry everything you might need. Those who try are the ones who leave things behind at the albergues early on or mail them ahead to Santiago. The rest must trust they will be able to find what they need along the way.

Karen, my wise friend from my first few days, told me a story of a woman she walked with the previous time she did the Camino. There was a special skin cream her companion had left at home, afraid it would just be one more thing to weigh down her pack. After some days of walking, she realized it would have been a helpful item to have brought along and would have soothed her aching feet. She expressed her regret at having not packed it. It was a brand not typically found in Spain. At the next albergue, there was a table with items left behind by other pilgrims—everything free for the taking. In the middle of the table was a container of the very cream the woman had wanted. When Karen told me this story, she concluded, "The Camino has a way of providing."

This kindness was harder to accept than I thought it would be. From the very first night, I received generosity from my fellow travelers. After the long slog in the rain to Roncevaux, a few of us washed our clothes and headed down to the laundry in search of a dryer. There were volunteers, who took our clothes and put them in the queue for drying. The service cost several Euros. A woman named Annemarie paid, and when I offered to chip in my half, she refused. I told her I would pay next time and, honestly, I felt a little uncomfortable not being able to reimburse her. As an American, I grew up in an independent and individualistic culture. We like to take care of ourselves and don't like to feel indebted to anyone. As a matter of fact, there was no next time, and I would not be able to return the favor. But I do not think Annemarie cared one bit. She was just being kind, sharing what she had.

For many people, myself included, kindness is easier to bestow upon others than it is to receive. The Camino gave opportunity to practice both, and each expression helped build the sense of community and family. Sharing of food might be the most comfortable expression of this, but there were others that felt far more intimate.

THE GOOD WAY

Walking five hundred miles puts a significant amount of stress on your body. Sooner or later, you will have aches, blisters, wounds, or injuries that need to be tended. Sometimes the help you need is as simple as a Band-Aid; other times you may need someone to lance a blister, clean a wound, or provide a little healing massage. The last three are far harder to accept from someone than a slice of cheese they just purchased. If you came with a friend, you may have your own built-in nurse, but if you started out alone, the only people you have to turn to are other travelers. A woman you did not know a few days ago might be doctoring a blister on your foot you simply cannot reach yourself.

This was literally true for me. I remember sitting on my bed trying to tend a hard-to-reach blister on my foot. My new friend Helen offered to help. Being an independent, self-reliant American, I said, "I think I can get it." Because of her own blisters, Helen had become an expert on blister care and had amassed her own blister-care kit. She picked up her tools, came over to my bed, and ordered me to prop up my foot. She reminded me of her newly developed expertise and proceeded to treat and bandage my blister. It was hard to sit there and allow her to do it. Part of me wanted to be self-sufficient, but another part appreciated the gracious care when I was in need. Similar acts of kindness, both large and small, made the transition from *strangers* to *family members* very natural on the Camino.

I could not help but think of the contrast typically experienced back home. There, I often walk through a park near my house, each time making a practice of smiling and saying good morning to everyone I pass. While some smile back and return the greeting, many pass by without making eye contact or even acknowledging my words.

Becoming Family

These people seem as if they have decided to shut off the opportunity for connection.

I did not experience this kind of guardedness on the Camino. For example, I saw a young lady several times in the towns where we had been staying. The group she traveled with kept pace with ours. I interacted with some of the people in her clan, but I had never had the opportunity to speak with her. Often, she and her group would leave a few minutes before us. Because I maintained a pretty quick pace, I would pass this young lady along the way. We would call out to one another "Buen Camino," or simply ask how the day was going, but we never had the opportunity to talk.

One day, I found myself again gaining on her, but when I came along side she began to match me stride for stride. I asked how her Camino was going and for the next two hours she shared what was on her heart, what issues God had brought up to her over the previous few weeks, how she was responding to His invitation, and how the whole experience had strengthened her faith in Christ. What a gift to have her share these things. When we reached the location where her group had planned to stop for lunch, we parted ways—but not before I thanked her for talking so openly and honestly.

Take that conversation and add to it the proximity of walking with someone or a group of people for days and weeks on end. There were numerous opportunities for significant relationships to be built in a short span of time. The conditions were ripe for strangers to become family, as people shared the experience of being loved, known, empowered, and released.

Some say the Camino is called *The Way* because on it you see a tangible expression of the way we are to live with and treat one another. For me, it was one of the most concrete expressions of the community described in the book of Acts that I have ever experienced:

> They devoted themselves to the apostles' teaching and to fellowship, to the breaking of bread and to prayer. Everyone was filled with awe at the many wonders and signs performed by the apostles. All the believers were together and had everything in common. They sold property and possessions to give to anyone who had need. Every day they continued to meet together in the temple courts. They broke bread in their homes and ate together with glad and sincere hearts, praising God and enjoying the favor of all the people. (2:42-47)

Nearly everyone I came across would find some time each day to be alone for prayer and meditation. We shared everything in common and gave to anyone who had need. We would meet together daily, along the trail, in our albergues, or around a table. Our hearts were glad and sincere. I think all of us were grateful, and I know I was not the only one praising God for the experience. We may not have seen the blind healed, but we did have our share of healing. I witnessed broken hearts mended and made whole, people enslaved by unforgiveness released, and the lonely brought into community.

For most people, any taste of community draws us in and captures our hearts. We are changed by it, making it difficult to return to our former independent, isolated, and self-reliant lives. At the time of this writing, it has been a month and a half since I have returned home. I remain in contact with many of those I walked with. When we had been home for a month, I sent a note to several, asking what it was like for them to be back for almost as long as they had walked. All of them spoke of how much of their heart was still captured by the Camino. They each shared ways they keep the experience present. One friend started walking to work, another keeps a collage of photos on her desk at work, another is already planning another trip abroad, and others are trying to live simpler lives so the lessons of the Camino won't be choked out by busyness. What all miss most are the relationships that were formed and the experience of living life as we did on the Camino on a daily basis.

On the Camino, I came across many people who were walking it for the second, third, or even fourth time. I believe people return so often because they experience community the way we were designed to live in it. Unfortunately, for most of us this is not true in our everyday lives. If we are lucky, we get glimpses of it, but often these are fleeting at best. In our daily lives, most of us do not live in the rhythm of community which is experienced on the Camino. How rich and rewarding it would be if we could live like this in our own neighborhoods, workplaces, and communities of faith.

Toward the end of the Camino journey, I found myself with a father and son, Mark and Sam. On our last night, Mark offered to make us pasta. He had shared several meals with an Italian man named Beppe. He was retired and liked hiking the Camino because it restored his hope in humanity. This was Beppe's fourth year in a row making the trek. Mark asked if he could watch as Beppe prepared dinner one night. As he cooked, they talked. Beppe seemed to enjoy the conversation and teaching Mark the process for making good pasta. Mark wanted to share his newly developed culinary expertise. We were delighted to let him.

As I watched him prepare the meal, I thought about the man who had taught him the skill. I could not help but wonder if Beppe's goal in returning to the Camino each year was far more significant than walking the distance or teaching others how to cook pasta. I wondered if he came back so often because the Camino was the only significant experience of community, outside of his family, he had each year. I imagined how it might feel to be waiting all year long so you could walk again and experience anew what it is to be loved, served, known, and released. I wondered what it would feel like for him, one day, to no longer be able to walk it.

I do not believe we are meant to experience this kind of community only once a year—or for some, once in a lifetime. I believe this is how we were intended to live on a daily basis. It is why I follow Jesus; living as He lived is the best hope for making it a reality. The questions all of us have to answer include: Are we willing to create the kind of space and simplicity to allow it to happen? Are we willing to learn to include, share, and listen? Are we willing to create environments where people are known, served, loved, and released?

The fact so many hearts are drawn to this kind of community gives me great hope that doing so is possible. Walking the Camino affirms my belief there are people who have the desire and capacity to make it happen.

Chapter Eight

LETTING GO

We had three wonderful days of walking together as a family before one of the realities of the Camino hit—saying goodbye. Marta and Yavidan had told us from the beginning that they were walking only so far. Yavidan was supposed to have already left the Camino, but the experience and the people were tugging on her heart, so she rearranged her travel plans to walk a bit farther. Now she would go as far as Burgos. Marta, on the other hand, could not adjust her plans. Knowing this was our last day of walking together, we spent most of the day keeping pace with one another. It was a beautiful day to walk through the vineyards and wheat fields that lined the path. Keeping a slow pace, it was as if we were savoring every moment with our friend Marta.

She had joined the group in Pamplona, though *joined* may be the wrong word to use. It was not like we were an exclusive group in which you had to obtain membership. We were a community open to anyone who might choose to walk with us, share a meal, and share their hearts. There were many families like this along the way. It was not a matter of being in or out, but of simply being *with*. What

THE GOOD WAY

Marta brought to our family was her passion for life. To watch her taste a delicious bite of food was to see her whole being enjoy it. She would close her eyes as if the flavor was transporting her to another place. Her body gently swayed as if the movement enabled her to better savor each morsel. Finally, she would utter a long "mmmm" sound and punctuate it with one simple word: "Delicious." A meal was an experience of life to Marta. What else would you expect, since she was Italian?

Being with Marta, the rest of us received an education in how to find enjoyment and pleasure in things we might normally be tempted to rush past. She brought joy and life to our journey. She made us smile, and there was much laughter in her voice. She also had one of the most amazing talents: She could unbuckle her pack, rotate it around her torso while removing her jacket, and buckle it back up without ever missing a stride. I begged her to let me post a video of it on YouTube to teach the rest of the world this unique technique. She smiled and then tried to give me a very stern look before saying, "No." Even her attempt to be firm only brought a smile to my face. She was a delight and added so much to our Camino family. I knew it was going to be hard to say goodbye.

Marta must have known it as well. A few kilometers before Santa Domingo, she told us she wanted to stop for a while. She was going to lay out a blanket and enjoy the beauty that surrounded the path. She wanted to take one last drink of it all before her walk was complete. I could not blame her.

The rest of us made our way into town and found our albergue, which was not open yet. We waited for about a half an hour before we could begin our normal routine of washing off the sweat and dirt from the morning's walk, cleaning our clothes, and heading out for a bite to eat. We found a nice square with several restaurants to choose from. Annemarie was there with a man named Josef. She had quickened her pace a few days earlier. I was surprised to see her again, expecting her to be a day ahead of us by now. I made sure we exchanged information just in case this was the last time we crossed paths. I had first seen Josef in St. Jean, and he was kind enough to give me his email as well. It would not be too long before others we had been walking with also arrived. Todd, Alice, and Dalia were akin to our first cousins. They were not intimate family as were the eight of us who walked together, but we often shared meals and conversation and enjoyed one another's company. Each time we would cross paths I felt the warmth of friendship and sense of belonging.

It had been some time since I'd had this experience. When Tammie and I were first let go from our church, we began attending a church thirty minutes from our home. It was the place where Tammie had taken the class where she was given the original vision of me being removed. The teaching was excellent and from what the pastor shared, his heart was in sync with ours regarding what it means to be a community of followers of Jesus.

Churches have books of worship. Some are vastly different from one another. This church's book was very similar to the one we had left. When we celebrated communion, they used the same exact trays as the church where we had celebrated it for the past thirty years. When we started attending, they were in the middle of a sanctuary remodel. When they finished, they had placed on the stage some of the same elements as our old church. All these things made it seem like home. The one big difference was size. This church was about six times larger than where we were coming from. This, along with the fact we lived a half hour away, made it difficult to enter into community. After eight months of attending the church, I did not know any more people than when I had begun. We needed to find something closer to home.

Tammie had been meeting with a pastors' wives group led by a woman named Megan. Because the others in the group were always so busy, often the only two people who would show up were Megan and Tammie. This was a gift. It allowed Tammie to be able to process what was taking place in our lives in a much deeper way than would otherwise be possible. It also allowed the relationship between Megan and Tammie to move from facilitator and group member to friends. Over the months, Tammie shared with her much of what was on our hearts regarding church and how we believed we ought to live out our identity in Christ in community. Megan was part of a team planting a church in our city and told Tammie she felt like the pastors of this new church were trying to live out much of what Tammie had shared. Megan thought we would be likeminded in many areas. These pastors would be launching the church in January, and she invited us to check it out. We decided to do so.

We did not realize the Sunday we attended was the week prior to their official launch. The pastor corrected our misconception when I met him at the end of the service. I shared a bit of our story. He suggested we get together for coffee and told me he would call. Knowing it was the week before their big event, I was surprised to get a call from him on Monday. I told him I knew what it was like to be getting ready for a big service and we could delay a week if he would rather. He responded, "We are more concerned about being the church than putting on a

Letting Go

perfect service. I have plenty of time to meet this week." I loved that attitude and wanted to be around it. It felt more like the kind of church where we were supposed to be.

We made the move to this new church and got involved in a home group. It felt good to be in a place where we were getting to actually know people. It was life giving to show up on a Sunday and have people know our names. It was still difficult to fully enter in. I was applying for positions at various churches and knew, even hoped, it would not be long before we would say goodbye and move on to the next place God had for us. We had been attending this new church for five months before I started walking the Camino. Even though we felt much more connected and known there, it did not compare to the feeling of belonging I now felt with those I was walking with. The bond of connection here seemed to be accelerated by the experience, proximity, and openness of the people. Having not experienced this fully since I left the church where I had served, I did not want it to come to an end.

While sitting in that square, we received a text from Marta. She was tossing out the ideas of moving on to the next town today but promised she would stop by to share one last glass of wine and to say goodbye. It was difficult for her to confront the fact her journey was ending. Because we were a persuasive bunch, after she arrived, we convinced her it would be much better to catch a bus to Burgos from Santa Domingo than from the next city. We talked about the joy of sharing one last meal together and then practically begged her to reconsider moving on. She stayed, but instead of getting a bed at the place we were staying, she chose to find one at another albergue. My guess is she wanted to avoid the tearful goodbye in the morning. It was just like her. Why depart in tears when you could leave with laughter shared around a meal?

After Marta settled into her home for the night, we spent the afternoon simply being with one another. Some of the time was savored sitting on the lawn behind her albergue; some spent wandering the town and touring the church. We did not talk of parting ways. While exploring the town, we came across the five Italian men I often walked with in the mornings. In the evenings, I often found them talking with Marta outside the albergues. I would sit among them, not understanding anything they said in their native tongue, but I enjoyed that their words were filled with life and laughter. We all gathered for a group photo. There were lots of smiles, not just for the photograph, but also because of the company and the sweetness of the moment. We headed off to dinner and then to bed. When we began walking the next morning, we were missing someone we had come to dearly love. I do not know how the others felt, but I felt the loss acutely.

Because Marta's absence began to stir something deep in me—even though I couldn't pinpoint what—I walked alone much of the next day. I wanted to be silent, listen to my own heart, and hear the voice of God. A few days earlier, I had walked alone in the morning along a particularly beautiful part of the Camino. Because it quickly dipped into several valleys and then back up to a ridge, I was able to witness three different sunrises that morning. As I walked, I talked to Jesus about the pain of how I was dismissed from my church and what it felt like. I heard Him say to me, "I know what it is to feel betrayed and discarded by those close to me. I chose to trust my Father, who is trustworthy. You can trust me and the one in whom I have placed my trust." All I could do that morning was practice walking in an attitude of trust. In the process, a peace fell over me.

Now feeling something stirring inside of me, I was hoping to once again hear Christ's voice and experience the same kind of serenity washing over me. But I did not hear Christ's voice as I walked, and I must not have felt peaceful because by the time I arrived at the village where we had planned to stay for the night, I was a full hour and a half ahead of the group. The first half hour of waiting was difficult. I started to wonder if they had decided to stop somewhere else. Could I have lost more than Marta that day? By the time I entered the second half hour of waiting, I was actively turning my heart to God, inviting Him into what I was feeling and asking for His peace in whatever the afternoon and evening might hold. Others I knew started to trickle into town, and a short time later my family finally arrived. There was someone new with them, Franziska. She was from Germany, spoke fluent Korean, and had a style about her that signaled she would be an interesting person to get to know. Sergio would not be far behind them.

We decided to make dinner together. The group had split into two different albergues and the one where Junyoung, Ki, and Franziska were staying had the best kitchen, so we would eat there. We arranged to meet up outside the church just before dinner to go shopping. While waiting for everyone to gather, people started to pull out their guidebooks to plan the next day's walk and determine when they would arrive in Santiago.

Franziska had someone she was trying to meet in Leon on a particular day. She would have to hustle if she hoped to get there in time. Junyoung and Ki were keen on speeding up, hoping to arrive in Santiago by the 27th.

THE GOOD WAY

Yavidan would be departing in Burgos. Emily would have family members meeting her in Santiago on the 29th. Samantha was shooting for that day as well, if not earlier. Sergio wanted to take forty days to walk the Camino and on to Finisterre. This meant he would need to slow down at some point. I had to meet a friend in Sarria on the 26th and knew this would put me into Santiago on the 30th. As I listened to each person discuss plans, I realized I would not be arriving in Santiago with any of them. They had become such an important part of my journey that I could hardly imagine it without them. I would walk farthest with Emily, but at some point we would be forced to say goodbye. My heart sank, and I did not have much appetite, but I still chose to savor the experience of our shared meal. I knew these opportunities would not last forever.

The next morning, I started out on my own. Whatever began stirring inside of me the day before was still present, and I wanted to allow it to surface. The map showed we had several closely spaced small towns to move through before we began longer sections through what appeared to be national forest. I moved quickly through the smaller villages, stopping at one to have breakfast. No café was open, so I sat down and pulled out the food I carried for just such emergencies. My stash consisted of an orange, peanuts and a bite or two of dark chocolate. I ate it while sitting outside of a picturesque church. The path up to this point had been relatively easy. It felt good to move quickly, but I had not yet been able to access what was going on in my heart. The movement through the villages and the short-distance goals they provided kept my mind on the pace and off what was going on internally. I was walking faster than at any time on the Camino thus far, but in some ways it felt as if I were going backward. By the

Letting Go

time I reached Villafranca Montes de Oca, I realized I needed to do more than move quickly—I needed to open my heart. I decided to pull out my iPod and listen to a mix of songs I had put together for our retreat in October, listening for God's voice regarding the future.

I was now climbing out of the wheat fields and into the mountains, on a steep incline leading out of the city. The music helped to take my mind off the burn in my lungs. It also helped me to begin to identify what had been stirring internally. The second song was titled "Worn," by Tenth Avenue North. By the second verse, I was weeping. The lyrics spoke of a soul which felt crushed by the weight of life and enduring hope that God could indeed bring rest. As the song cried out to see redemption rule the day, my heart also sung out its own desire for healing. I longed for God to mend my torn heart and to see this struggle end.

As I allowed the words of the song to wash over me a floodgate was opened. I was not just crying but sobbing. With my ear buds in and the music drowning out all other sound, I could not tell if the Italian men I had been walking with on most mornings were behind me. For a moment, I wondered what they would think of the crazy American blubbering on the trail, but I pushed it out of my mind. I did not care. Something deep inside of me bubbled to the surface and began to be released. To stay in the moment, I hit the replay button and listened to the song several more times. This was not about Marta's leaving or even the eventual departure of all of my Camino family. It was about home, the church where I served, the people I love, and how it all ended.

One of the people who journeyed with me through that painful season was my spiritual director. Long before I was ever let go, we processed together what it was like to walk in humility through the transition. She said to me, "Death comes before resurrection, but resurrection will come." The last two years had made me feel very worn and crushed. I had become familiar with loss, feeling the "death" of many important things in my life. I longed for the redemption this song cried out for.

As I walked, I allowed myself to daydream about what my personal and spiritual resurrection might look like. I imagined being back with the people I loved, living life with them, serving them, having all of this hurt healed, and experiencing redemptions together. Specific individuals crossed my mind, and I imagined living in community with them again. Through tears, I would catch myself smiling.

These, however, were just wish-dreams. It was not going to happen, but it was still worth imagining. Allowing myself to daydream about what could have been also allowed me to acknowledge the deepest desires of my heart. In this moment, I could recognize them for what they were, grieve what was lost, and let them go. I was dying to some of my heart's deepest longings—maybe not fully, but in a way I had not allowed myself to do before. I would have rather held on to them, but I knew walking here in the presence of my Creator, He was inviting me to release what, in truth, I had no capacity to hold on to.

The songs that followed spoke of the voice of truth, and the need for healing and hope. In my mind, I was burying my wish-dreams along the path and asking God to help me recognize truth and experience hope. The tears had stopped and what had been stirring in my heart for some time now felt released. Surrounded now by forest, I noticed the smell of pine in the air. Birds filled the trees. The songs they sang made their way past my ear buds and seemed to harmonize with the music. I walked slower, observing flowers that lined the pathway and butterflies that darted about. I thought about beauty and the process of transformation—how flowers, butterflies, and many other of God's creations must struggle to emerge into something beautiful.

I arrived at St. Juan de Ortega an hour before my family. There was a festival going on in the village, and it was crowded. I saw a field filled with barbeques, tables, and chairs just before I entered the village. People started to gather in front of the church, festivities were about to begin with a processional. When the others arrived, we decided to step out of the commotion and move on to the next town, Ages. Even though my body was tired, I knew there would be great joy in walking the additional 3.6 kilometers to the next albergue together. Along the way, we walked under a cloud-filled sky that seemed to stretch on forever. We laughed, sang, marveled at the beauty, and simply enjoyed being present with one another.

The next day we made our way to Burgos. This was the final leg of the journey for Yavidan. It was a Sunday, and the sunrise we were treated to provided an appropriate context for worship. I felt profound gratitude for what God was doing in me and the people He had surrounded me with on this journey. Knowing it was Yavidan's last day of walking, I asked her what she had learned along the way. She told me she had discovered she was beautiful even without makeup. For a woman who makes her living in the fashion industry, this was much more significant than discovering she could get by without mascara. I had to agree, she indeed was a beautiful person, even without makeup. I was grateful to have gotten acquainted with her and for her willingness to share her heart.

THE GOOD WAY

The next morning Yavidan popped out of bed just long enough to give us a hug and say goodbye, before we continued on. She was going to get more sleep because she was catching a bus later in the day. I had walked with her from day one, and now we were saying goodbye. I had not walked any part of the Camino without her and I was sad to see her go, but it was different than saying good-bye to Marta. I was learning to let go without it taking away anything from the experiences we had shared together. I was discovering what it meant to walk on. Two days later, I would be able to exercise this capacity once more.

* * *

The day after Burgos, we passed by our planned stop of Hornillos del Camino and made our way to Hontanas. It was our longest daylong trek so far, 31.8 kilometers. The last eleven kilometers were made even more difficult because we had entered the Meseta. The terrain was flat and unchanging. Unlike most villages where the church bell tower can be seen from far away, Hontanas is nestled in a valley with no sign of it until you are right upon it. All we could see were miles and miles of fields before us. Without any landmarks, it was impossible to judge how far we still had to go. I knew what kind of distance I would cover in an hour, but if I were keeping my normal pace, we should have been there already. The extra eleven kilometers we decided to walk were the longest of the Camino for me.

The only thing that made the trek bearable was walking with Ki. We had spent much time together and enjoyed each another's company, but this was the first time we had been alone with the chance to talk uninterrupted. He asked why I was walking the Camino, and I told him about the past two years and what God has been doing in my heart. I shared the pain of being cleaved from community and what a gift he had been to me. I also was able to talk to him about why I had become a pastor and why I chose to follow Jesus. It was an effortless and natural conversation that revealed how comfortable we had become with each another.

After arriving in Hontanas, Ki and Junyoung decided to cook for us. The only kitchen the albergue had was also used to cook and serve the pilgrim's meal offered by the establishment. There was a small table in the kitchen that was perfect for the six of us. We spent our evening helping Junyoung and Ki in any way we could and dodging the albergue's staff as they came in to use the facilities as well. It was late by the time we sat down to eat, but that did not stop us from lingering around the table. We did not realize it at the time, but it would be the last dinner we would share together. Tomorrow, our group would once again shrink, this time by half. Fourteen days into the journey, not even halfway done, and our Camino family, would essentially be dissolved.

Chapter Nine

CREATED SPACE

As we headed out of Hontanas, we needed to decide where we would stay for the night. Because we had gone farther than anticipated the day before, stopping in Castrojeriz, our planned destination would make for a short day. For Franziska, who was trying to get to Leon by June 15, this was perfect because it would allow her to cover more distance. Junyoung and Ki were also up for pressing on. Samantha, Emilie, and I were undecided. We had at least a two-hour walk until we got to Castrojeriz, where we would take a break for café con leche, and then have to make our choice.

I had asked Emilie to encourage me to walk slower. It was not that she was slow necessarily; often she would arrive in a town only ten to twenty minutes behind me. When she walked, however, she did not seem to be as rushed as I often felt. My knees had been hurting, and I wondered if my fast pace had contributed. I had also wanted to learn to be more present in the moment, rather than having my thoughts occupied with how soon I would arrive at the next location.

My goal was to walk beside or behind Emilie. It

sounded easy enough, but it was much harder than I imagined. We would go on just fine for a bit, but inevitably I would find myself moving out in front of her. It would take me a moment to become aware of this. I would finally catch myself and then return to her side or allow her to pass. I found it difficult to walk at any pace that was not my normal stride. Emilie was patient, never pointing out my propensity to move ahead. She simply kept her pace and allowed me to fall back when I had noticed I'd taken the lead.

As I have endeavored to follow God in this season of life and ministry, much of walking through this transition has felt like learning the same lessons. There are times I find myself falling into the rhythm of my own pace and getting out ahead of God. I do not always recognize it immediately, but eventually I realize God is not out in front, and I must fall back in line behind Him. He is patient with me, as Emilie was. He keeps His pace and is gracious enough to allow me to return when I notice I have wandered from my role as follower. The exercise of allowing Emilie to disciple me in walking slowly was a physical manifestation of what God had been forming in me over the past two years. It was also a reminder of how much I still have to learn.

As we walked, Emilie and I talked about this book and what it would be about. I told her I did not completely know yet. I was allowing the experience of the Camino to help form and shape it. This led us to talk about our attitudes regarding the things that happen to us. Often, when we find ourselves standing at the crossroads, we want to know which way we are to go. We are eager to move, especially if we perceive our circumstances as bad. We pondered together what it would be like to set aside our desire to determine our next move and instead focus on how our circumstances are shaping us. Maybe what's most important is not what comes next or discerning where to go, but who we are becoming in the process. I shared with her my desire to be so rooted and grounded in my identity in Christ that I became the kind of person who has the capacity to love no matter the circumstances. This is hard, I admitted—almost as hard as walking slowly, I added with a smile—but it is what God is trying to teach me in during this season.

As we talked about these things, it felt very much like we were living in the present moment. This is a rhythm the Camino seems to draw you into as you walk. Emilie and I talked about what it would be like to live this way at home, where there are so many distractions and diversions. We shared some ideas, but did not have any real answers. We were, however, carrying a growing desire to live in this same rhythm in our everyday lives.

Approaching the town, we could see the ruins of an old castle that stood on a hill above it. The guidebook said it was well worth the strenuous climb to explore its towers. We stopped at the first open bar for café con leche. It took a few minutes before all of us were sitting around the table. Our friend Karen, who had surprisingly shown up at our albergue the night before, had stopped as well. Her arrival just before we went to sleep had been an unexpected gift. Now sitting together, we enjoyed the coffee, pastries, and the rest that our morning ritual afforded.

Several of us took out our guidebooks and started to weigh our options for the day. Should we stay or move on? We said goodbye to Karen for the final time as she set off. We went around the table and asked what each person was going to do. Samantha wanted to stay. She thought the castle was worth exploring in the afternoon. Emilie was on the fence at first, but then decided on stopping. Franziska, Junyoung, and Ki decided to continue. For me, either choice would bring loss. I would either be choosing to leave some of the family behind or watch a few of its members walk away. I did not want either, but since I would arrive in Santiago later than all of them, I was in no hurry. A partial day of rest almost halfway into our journey seemed to be a good decision. I chose to stay. I snapped one last photo of our three friends and then watched them walk off.

We had several hours before the albergue opened, which would allow us to stow our packs and explore the castle. So we spent the morning journaling, writing postcards, and checking out the town. It was a much different pace than we were used to at this time of day. Once the albergue opened, we settled our stuff and went to explore the ruins. The climb was steep, but made easier without our packs. The views were spectacular, and the steel reinforcements and walkways made it possible to explore and climb throughout the castle. All three of us were pleased with our decision to stop. It created the space necessary to enjoy this town in a way our normal rhythm of walking would not have allowed. I was sorry we could not share it with Franziska, Junyoung, and Ki.

As we made our way back down to the village, we came across Todd. He had just arrived in Castrojeriz and was planning to pass through quickly. He had left us a couple of days earlier, telling us he wanted to make better time. I had not expected to see him again. I asked him, "How in the world do you keep getting behind us?" He filled us in on what he had been up to the past few days, and then said he needed to get moving. We tried to convince him to stop for the night, arguing he would probably just end up behind us in a day or two anyhow, but he insisted he needed to press on.

Not long after saying goodbye to Todd, Sergio made his way into town. He had stopped at our original destination the day before. Because we had moved on, we had been separated for one night. Our albergue was already full so he had to stay in another. After he got settled, he met us at our albergue. We had a patio where we could hang out and have Wi-Fi access, which was not provided where he was staying. We sat at the picnic benches on the patio connecting with home on our smart phones and conversing with one another in between texts and Facebook posts.

A little earlier in the day, three women arrived at the albergue. They were some of the last to check in before it was full. They were from New Zealand and had begun their Camino in Burgos. This was their second day of walking. Sergio had met them the night before in Hornillos del Camino.

Two of them were heading out to explore a spot they had seen as they entered the city. Sergio invited the third woman, Helen, to sit with us. Though I have mentioned her early, this was actually the first time we met. Like her traveling companions, she was twenty-three years old. I quickly learned she taught preschool back at home in Auckland. I told her I taught a course in seminary that explores how we are formed spiritually in community and the importance of early relational experiences in developing our ability to attach to God. I shared some of the concepts we discuss in class, and she gave examples of them from her experiences with preschoolers.

THE GOOD WAY

Time passed quickly, and someone brought up the subject of when and where we were going to eat. The kitchen at the albergue was sparse, so we decided to eat out. Samantha, Emilie, Sergio, myself and now Helen found a local hotel and settled in for dinner. Since Helen was new, it seemed natural to ask questions about her life and reasons for walking the Camino. She was open and honest with us about why she had come. She had recently dealt with some significant loss. It had caused a ripple effect of pain, not only for her, but also in the lives of others who were close to her. As she talked, it felt as if she were allowing us to walk on the holy ground of her experience.

As she shared the circumstances surrounding the situation and how she was dealing with them, I could not help but think, *If she was my daughter, I would be extremely proud of how she's handling herself.* I felt as if God was prompting me to speak out loud what I was thinking, but I was not sure how she would respond. After all, I barely knew her. Unable to shake the prompting, I finally said, "Helen, I have known you for only a few hours, so this may not mean very much to you, but I would like to say something as someone who is about the same age as your parents: After listening to you share what has been going on in your life and how you are walking through it, I am very proud of you and how you are handling yourself. If my daughter had to go through what you are experiencing, I would hope she would be as strong as you have been." Her response was simple and genuine. She said, "Thank you." I had a sense it struck a chord in her heart. It felt like an ordained moment.

We finished dinner soon after and began to walk back to the albergue. I stopped the group and asked if I could

Created Space

snap a photo. I wanted a picture to remind me of what had taken place at this meal. I knew God was at work in Helen's life, and I had been privileged to be part of what He was doing, at least for this moment.

* * *

The next day, Emilie began the hard work of once again discipling me in walking slowly. The climb out of Castrojeriz was steep, so it was not difficult to keep my pace slow in this section. I had a hard time imagining Todd making this climb late in the day. We had started early, but not as early as Samantha, who was long gone.

While I had walked with Emilie longer than anyone, we were still getting to know each another. We talked about books and movies that had influenced us. We talked about what it takes to overcome obstacles in life and about our lives back home. The conversation was easy, and it made the kilometers pass quickly. Every now and then, we would pause to take in a particularly beautiful view. More than once I would notice I was out in front and I would have to move beside or fall in behind Emilie once again. Somewhere around kilometer ten, we stopped for a café con leche. After our break, we decided to walk alone the rest of the way. I put on my iPod and listened to Bebo Norman, whose song "Big Blue Sky" seemed appropriate as I walked under the hot Spanish sun.

Our destination for the day was Fromista. By midafternoon we were all there, Samantha, Emilie, Sergio, and myself. Present also were the three young ladies from New Zealand, three young men from the States who had been tracking with us for some time, and several other new faces. We spent the afternoon sitting under the shade in the courtyard, writing postcards and getting better acquainted. The day had brought us 25.2 kilometers closer to Santiago and was providing an opportunity to grow closer to those with whom we were now walking.

Once closed for the night, the door to the albergue was locked until six-thirty the next morning. There was a line of us waiting to depart when it was finally opened. Because of this, Samantha, who usually got a head start on us each morning, decided to walk with Emilie and me. Samantha walked very quickly, while I was still learning to walk slower. I do not know what Emilie was thinking or at whose pace we were walking, but we stayed relatively close together throughout the morning. We were not too far into the day before the ladies from New Zealand, whom we had dubbed the Kiwis, passed us. A little farther down the road, we found them taking a break to eat breakfast, and we decided to join them. We would end up walking together the rest of the day.

As we neared our next destination, Carrion de Los Condes, one of the Kiwis named Rachel and I walked together. By now our group had spread out a bit, and she and I were at the head of the column (so much for learning to walk slowly). I shared what had led me to make this journey and asked about her reason. She, like her friend Helen, came to the Camino with her own experience of loss and hurt. She also had a strong desire to be present with herself as she walked and to be open to what might need to change. She had come with the desire to think through some of the bigger questions of life.

We did not notice how far we had gotten out in front of the others. By the time we arrived at the edge of town, they were well behind us. I went on to the albergue to see if I could find Sergio, as he had pressed on in front of us earlier in the day and offered to hold spots for us. Rachel decided to wait for the others to make their way into town. As we parted, I thanked her for the conversation and said I was sure we would talk again. She said she had been feeling down, but now was feeling better and was also thankful for the chat. It was wonderful to see how simply sharing our stories could lift our spirits.

After we were all settled, Sergio and I found a bar with free Wi-Fi access so we could email our wives. While we sat there, Rachel came and sat down. She mentioned my conversation with Helen a few nights before and how much it had impacted her. This led us to pick up where we had left off in the morning, talking about life, relationships, and faith. It was a wonderful thing to have the time to sit and be present to what the Spirit of God was stirring in the heart of another. After an hour or so, Rachel headed back to the albergue and I headed down to the river.

I found Todd sitting by the river. He was supposed to be days ahead of us, but here we were once again in the same town. I asked him what he had been up to since I had last seen him. He told me about his experiences and how he ended up in the town at this time. He also said he would be continuing on. Three times I had said goodbye to him, and three times he had shown back up. I knew at some point this good fortune would come to an end. He needed to arrive in Santiago three days before me and he now had to squeeze eighteen days of walking into fifteen. I wondered what God might be up to in allowing us to continue to cross paths.

I enjoyed Todd and his perspective on life and ministry. He was currently serving as a prison chaplain. We shared many of the same convictions of what we are

THE GOOD WAY

called to be as followers of Jesus. As I listened to him recount the last few days of his Camino, I asked God to reveal to me why we kept finding each other. It occurred to me that God might be using Todd to speak about what He was calling me to. I also wondered how God would want to use me in Todd's life. Without any specific prompting, I tried to affirm Todd for who he was and what he does. Soon, he said goodbye, walked over the bridge, and headed out of town.

* * *

I returned to the river with Sergio later in the afternoon to soak my feet. It was something he and I had made a practice of in every town that had a river. As I approached the riverbank, I noticed the third Kiwi, Amy, sitting out in the sun. I said hello as I passed her. I found a place at the edge of the river, removed my sandals, and dipped my feet into the flowing water. The wind was gently blowing through the cottonwood trees on the edge of the river, causing them to release their fuzz. The white wisps danced and swirled in the breeze until they finally came to rest on the surface of the water, joining what seemed to be a cotton boat race driven by the current.

After just a few moments of taking in this scene, I noticed I was not alone. Amy had gotten up and came over to sit next to me. We had engaged in snippets of conversation over the past couple of days but had never really talked. Now our conversation began with observations about the fuzz floating in the wind and on the water. It was not long before Amy mentioned my conversation with Helen. It was the second time in one day it was used as a way to wade into deeper waters. God seemed to be doing more with the moment I had shared with Helen at the restaurant than I would have ever imagined.

I was not surprised to find Amy was also bringing to the Camino her own hurt and loss. Maybe we all were. We talked about the details of what she had experienced and how she was growing because of it. We sat there, amid the falling fuzz, our feet dangling in the river, talking about relationships, how they affect us, and how we can love. Every now and then, someone would jump into the cold water, making a big splash and interrupting the cadence of our conversation. As the ripples of water settled back into the surface of the river, we would settle back into our discussion. Eventually, Sergio came over and told us how a snake swam through his legs just a few meters downstream. It seemed like an appropriate time to end the conversation and start preparing for dinner.

As we walked back toward our albergue, I thought about the new people who had been introduced to our Camino family. I thought about how wonderful it was to be at an age when I was seen as a father figure and perceived as safe enough to open up to. I thought back to the morning when we all had sat at the table, deciding whether to stay in Castrojeriz or move on. I knew if I had decided to move on, I would not have been used by God to speak healing words to Helen or been available to listen to Rachel and Amy. These conversations seemed to be much more than people getting acquainted. There was a feeling of expectancy around what God was doing and how He was weaving these interactions together.

There was more. I could not help but wonder what would have happened if my three family members, whom I had grown to dearly love, had stayed. Would there have been space at the table for Helen? Would there have been room for the conversation with Rachel to take place as we walked? Would I have already been talking with someone else alongside the river? It seemed to me, as I thought about it, as important as my decision to stay was in forming these new relationships, the decision Franziska, Junyoung, and Ki made to keep walking was as equally important. In moving on, they created space in which these new relationship could grow.

This was a huge paradigm shift for me. I had always thought, and even verbalized to others, that I never wanted anyone to ever leave the circle of relationship. I desired it to be ever growing and expanding, a place where there was always space for new people—but I did not ever want anyone to ever leave. Being at the same church for twenty-nine years, I had seen a lot of people move on and I had seen many new people enter in. I always celebrated when new folks became part of our family, and I always grieved when anyone left, no matter the reason. The first circumstance seemed natural and good; the latter seemed unnatural and bad. Like the world being subjected to death after the Fall, loss of people from the community seemed like a consequence of things not being ordered as originally intended. I had never considered that someone moving on from the community might actually be creating the space necessary for others to enter in.

How the three moved on was vitally important to being able to shift the paradigm and seeing it as a good. They were not pushed out. They did not leave angry. They did not go because the community was unloving. There were no unresolved issues to unpack, no forgiveness to extend and be received, and no hurt feelings being held on to. They simply had another schedule to keep, another calling to respond to. While their leaving created space at the table for others, the circle of fellowship remained unbroken. They departed in peace and in the hope the Camino might yet bring us back together.

I would not say my departure from my church was rooted in the same peace or unbroken fellowship. There are hurts to be healed, unresolved issues to be unpacked, and forgiveness to be extended and received. I do not have the power, nor am I in the position, to bring all of this about. But I must be willing. I must also be open to the real possibility the space created by the loss of relationship, no matter how it has come about, may be exactly what is necessary to provide opportunity for other relationships to be birthed and grown. Since my departure, I had been holding on to the wish-dream of seeing all of it restored. Now, I was coming to recognize, as hard as it was to see these people removed from my immediate circle, the space created might be what was necessary to allow for ordained moments to occur, like the ones I had experienced in the last few days.

I was beginning to believe that the space created in the circle didn't need to be viewed as loss and letting go, but as an invitation to openness and preparation to receive. My view of how tightly we are to hold on to relationships, verses how open we ought to be to allowing them to change, was growing and maturing. Instead of walking in grief, I found myself beginning to walk in anticipation of what God might be up to and who He would bring into our Camino family—and into my life when I returned home.

Chapter Ten

WILDERNESS AND STONES

The word *meseta* is translated into English as the word *plateau*. Literally it means "table mountain" or "tablelands." In Spain, this word refers to the elevated, flat land that stretches over nearly 40 percent of the country. After the strenuous climb over the Pyrenees and the elevation gains and losses that lead into Burgos, you would think a long stretch of relatively flat land would be a welcomed sight. But for many pilgrims, it is not the case. The Meseta is not only flat, but it is also largely treeless and windblown. In the summer it can be scorching hot, and in the winter it can be bone-chillingly cold. While there is a distinct beauty to the wheat and barley crops swaying in the wind, much of the path through this region is dry and dusty.

Walking kilometer after kilometer in what appears to be an unchanging landscape can become monotonous. Many have characterized this section of the Camino as desolation. The prospect of walking long distances in a barren landscape—with no place to find relief from the sweltering sun and blowing dust—for many pilgrims does not seem worth the physical and mental energy required to make the trek. On the forum pages that give advice to first-time pilgrims, there are many who have no qualms granting permission to simply avoid this section altogether by taking a bus from Burgos to Leon or Astorga. They offer justifications like, "It is your Camino experience, and if you want to avoid this barren, arid landscape in order to spend your time in the more beautiful sections of the Camino, who is to tell you it's wrong?"

They are right, of course—it is your Camino experience. Walk it as you like, but before you make your final decision, you need to know the Meseta offers more than dusty trails, scorching sun, and seemingly unchanging scenery. There is something magical about how the sky and land work together to allow you to see distant objects with sharpness and clarity. It is precisely because of this effect that I was looking forward to walking through the Meseta, rather than avoiding it.

I was not hoping to see distant church spires and castle towers with great clarity; instead, I wanted the land's desolation to allow me to see God clearly and to gain perspective on His work during this season of my life. Much like Moses' experience in the wilderness, I hoped walking through this section of the Camino might attune my ears and eyes to God's presence. I had sensed His whisper earlier on the Camino, and now I was hoping He would show up in a *burning bush*. I did not see the Meseta as an invitation into desolation, but an opportunity to potentially walk on holy ground.

One unexpected consequence of walking through this barren land was that it caused our family to bond together in a way not required before. The conditions in the mountains allowed us to start at any time and walk well into the day. By midmorning in the Meseta it was hot and uncomfortable enough to keep us from wanting to walk farther. In order to avoid the heat of the day, our little clan began setting out before sunrise.

We were fortunate to have arrived in the region at the time of month when the full moon appeared. This made walking before dawn much easier than it would have been otherwise. We would start as early as five o'clock. For the first hour and a half, only the light of the moon illuminated the path. There was enough light to see where we were going, but not enough to keep us from searching in the dark for the yellow arrows and shells that pointed the way to Santiago. While the light-colored stone and dust on the dirt roads reflected the moon's light, it was still hard to judge the depth of depressions and potholes that littered the path. All of this caused us to stick closer together than we might have if we were still walking in the mountains. This proximity provided the opportunity for amazing conversations about life, faith, and what we were uniquely created to do.

Our conversations were not merely the exchange of ideas and ideologies. We talked about some of the deepest questions of our hearts and shared some of the most broken places that have marred our souls. We spoke of hope and growth, and how these things can be used by God to create something new. We provided a mirror for one another so we could see ourselves more clearly and perhaps closer to how God does. We shared with one another the things that we found beautiful and moved our hearts deeply. On more than one occasion, someone would pull out their phone to play a song that touched their soul or to read an inspiring quote.

All of these conversations were held in place by walking in long periods of silence. We had reached the depth of relationship where we could be engaged in conversation one moment and then walk alongside one another in silence the next. Sometimes, as I was walking in silence, thinking about the conversation we had just shared, I found myself smiling at the ease with which we were able to enter into these moments of sharing that drilled down to the core of who we were. These conversations often would begin with a simple question or observation. They were invitations for the other person to be known and loved.

In his book *The Meaning of Marriage*, Tim Keller describes the difference this experience can make in a relationship:

> To be loved but not known is comforting but superficial. To be known and not loved is our greatest fear. But to be fully known and truly loved is, well, a lot like being loved by God. It is what we need more than anything. It liberates us from pretense, humbles us out of our self-righteousness, and fortifies us for any difficulty life can throw at us.

What Keller describes as necessary for marriage is really necessary for any relationship where the love of God is manifested. Though I had not yet seen any burning bushes in the Meseta, God was using my companions to provide a tangible experience of what it is to be loved by Him. There was no fear, and it was not superficial. This did, as Keller suggests, liberate us from our pretense and humble us out of our self-righteousness. These were heavy weights to leave along the way, and we walked lighter because of it.

While many see the Meseta as desolation, I was finding

it to be full of life. I had entered it expecting to be alone with God and hear Him speak. What I was experiencing was what it is to be in a community where I was known and loved—and where I knew and loved others. For all of us, this was fortifying us, not only for the difficulties we were currently experiencing, but also to face the difficulties we carried with us as we came to the Camino.

It was taxing on our bodies and minds to make our way through this hot, dry land. It was just as taxing to hold on to the losses and broken relationships most of us had experienced before we set foot on the Way. Our experience of walking together was strengthening us and giving us the courage to be able to release much more than our pretense and self-righteousness. We were being lead to the path of forgiveness. Walking upon it would truly set us free.

* * *

While some would say that Leon marks the end of the Meseta, if you look on a map you will see the path does not begin climbing into the mountains again until after Astorga. For us, this would signify the end of our journey through the Meseta. The walk in to the town was dry, hot, and long. Rachel and I were once again at the front of the group. We paired up midway through the day's journey and walked the last sixteen kilometers together. We shared some significant discussions and kept one another going by playing twenty questions and posing riddles. Just about the time we were ready to give up, a small stand with free fruit, snacks, and drinks appeared on the trail. The owners would accept donations but were just as happy to allow people to take what they wanted for free. This oasis energized us for the last few kilometers—or at least that is what we thought until we began the long slog through the town leading up to Astorga and the climb into the city itself. There was even a pedestrian bridge over the train tracks that seemed to add a whole kilometer to the journey. By the time we arrived at the albergue, we were beat.

It took a while until we all arrived and settled into our room. Rachel disappeared for a few moments, returning to announce that she, Helen, Amy, and Rolando would be taking a rest day in Astorga. They had originally planned on stopping in Leon two days earlier but were not ready to let the rest of the family walk off. Now, after the punishing day on the road, they felt it was best to stop for a day and rest. I told them it sounded like a good decision. Rachel asked me to consider staying, but I told them I had arranged to meet someone on the 26th of June and did not want to burn my one rest day in case I needed it later.

It was hard to think about walking away from them, but I had learned by now the Camino would reunite us if it were meant to be. All we could do now was enjoy our last afternoon and evening together. We bought lunch items and ate in the albergue's dining room. We then made plans for dinner and spent the rest of the afternoon resting, exploring, and enjoying one another's company.

Just before dinner, Rachel and I walked down to the supermarcado to get last-minute supplies. On our way back to the albergue, we passed a park and she asked if I would like to go take a look. On one side there was a wall that overlooked the lower city. We sat on the wall, took in the view, and began to talk.

Some of the most significant conversations I had shared along the Way had been with Rachel. There was much going on in her heart and mind. I felt privileged she had shared so much of it with me; I also knew there were parts she was holding back. Now, as we sat there on the wall, she began to talk openly about things she had only hinted at in our earlier conversations. Then she would talk about them as semi-hypothetical situations; now she was revealing some of her deepest hurts and fears. I knew this was indeed holy ground.

As I listened to her, I was reminded of a woman who had sought me out for spiritual direction. She wanted guidance in how to forgive someone who had wounded her years ago. She realized her unforgiveness was harming her relationship with her husband. What prompted her to come and see me was a sermon I had preached on forgiveness six months earlier. I told her I did not have a magic formula to make her hurt go away, but I would be glad to help her explore how God was moving in her life. We met once a month for a year, initially sifting through the origin of her woundedness. In the eighth month, she said God had helped her to see something with great clarity: She did not want to let go of her unforgiveness. She likened it to a backpack she had been carrying around for years. It was heavy and cumbersome, but strangely enough, it was comfortable and provided a sense of security. In some ways, she *liked* carrying her unforgiveness.

I was amazed at the insight God had brought to her but knew quoting a few verses about how we are to forgive would not bring the healing she desperately desired. Since God had brought her this far, I was confident He would bring her all the way home. I looked up at the top shelf in my office, where I kept rocks I had taken from peaks I have climbed. I picked a stone and handed it to her. I asked her if she would be willing to carry this rock in her purse, letting it represent the unforgiveness she had been carrying around. Every time she picked up her purse and felt the weight, she should simply pray, "Jesus, help me to let go of my unforgiveness and choose to forgive." She was willing to accept my challenge and left my office with her purse a little heavier than when she arrived.

A month later, she came into my office, sat down, immediately reached into her purse, and handed me the rock. I refused to take it. I explained that she had carried her backpack for a long time, and I was pretty sure she would not be able to set it down in one month. She just smiled at me, insisted I take the rock, and told me how the Spirit of God had led her to be able to forgive over the previous month. We met for another few months to follow up on what had taken place. She indeed was a different person—she had found freedom.

I shared this story with Rachel, who seemed intrigued, so I told of another experience. At a summer camp where I served as a pastor, we once had an exercise on forgiveness early in the week. We had the children write on a rock the name of a person or a situation they needed to forgive. We then encouraged them to take the rock and toss it into the woods, symbolizing their willingness to extend forgiveness. One little girl wrote the name of her dad, who had abandoned the family, but she was unwilling to toss it into the woods. She was unwilling to forgive. Her counselor wisely allowed the girl to keep the rock. In fact, she carried it around much of the week. It was a reminder of the unforgiveness she was carrying. God continued to work on the girl's heart, and by Friday she was ready to forgive and left the stone at the cross we hiked to at the end of camp each year.

The next morning when the girl's mother arrived, she could tell something had changed in her daughter. The anger she carried with her no longer seemed to be present. As they drove out of camp, she started asking questions about what had taken place. By the time they reached the freeway, the daughter was relaying how she had forgiven her father, telling her mom she needed to forgive him too. Tears began to flow down the mother's face, and within a few miles she had to pull over because she was crying too hard to drive. There, on the side of the I-5 freeway, she chose to forgive her ex-husband. She wanted to experience what she could so clearly see in her daughter. The car had come to camp a week earlier with two people who were burdened by the weight of unforgiveness. They were now returning home free.

I told Rachel that in two days I would be climbing to the highest point of the Camino, Cruz de Ferro. She would reach it the day after me. On that spot stands an iron cross. People have carried stones to the place for centuries and left them as a symbol of leaving behind their sins or burdens in preparation for the final part of the journey into Santiago. I told her about the stone I had carried from a beach in California. I had collected it and many others just like it, all shaped by the sand and surf into round, smooth stones. They looked almost identical. I told her they reminded me of how God uses all the hard things in our lives to shape us into the image of Christ, the one who loves and forgives, if we are willing. Nothing is wasted. Each abrasive grain of sand and each wave that tosses us along the shore is redeemed by God, who will mold us into the person we were created to be.

I realized it was not just Rachel I had been speaking

to—it was also myself. I needed to be willing to lay down my stone at the cross, releasing into Christ's hands my hurt, wounds, and any unforgiveness I held on to. Cruz de Ferro would be making itself available to both of us.

We had been sitting on the stone wall, discussing stones, for more than an hour. It felt like all of our conversations over the past nine days had been leading up to this one. On one hand, I hated the ideas of walking away from all of them in the morning, on the other, it felt as if it had all been ordained and I had the freedom to hold it all loosely and move on.

***

In 1 Kings 19, we encounter Elijah fleeing into the wilderness, his life being threatened by Jezebel. He was tired and worn. The wilderness was a place to escape. After collapsing under a broom tree, he asked God to be released from his suffering through death. The Lord did not grant Elijah's request. Instead, God sent angels to attend to him. They knew the journey was too much for Elijah. He could not continue in His own power—he needed to be revived. The angels provided him with nourishment and allowed Elijah to rest. Eventually, he was strong enough to continue his journey for another forty days until he came to Horeb, the mountain of God. There, he heard God's voice, not in a powerful wind, earthquake, or raging fire, but in a whisper. The Lord told Elijah to go back to where he had come from, instructing him on what he was to do once he arrived.

The circumstances were still the same. Jezebel was still gunning for him. Elijah's experience in the wilderness, on the other hand, had changed something inside of him. God had met Elijah in his weakness and nourished him. God had whispered what Elijah needed to know to move forward. The next section of Scripture begins with three simple but powerful words: "So Elijah went." It was enough to lift him out of his despair and return him to the road God had laid out for him.

I had not been seeking death as a release when I entered the Meseta. I was, however, worn and seeking to hear from God. I wanted a burning bush. The Lord did not give me what I desired. Instead, God sent His messengers in the form of new family members. They were in some ways as worn as I was, but as we walked together, we received the nourishment and rest we needed to continue the journey. Walking with them, I heard God's voice in a whisper. "This is what I have made you to do: Partner with me in creating environments where people can be known and loved, spaces where they can be healed and set free. Go from this place and do what I have made you to do."

The next morning I went. Those of us who were continuing on sought to quietly slip out of the albergue, we said goodbye to the Kiwis and Rolando. There were brief hugs, well wishes, and gratitude for having shared this part of the journey. As I walked through the dimly lit streets with Emily and Allison, who had joined us in Leon, I thought to myself, *If my Camino ended today, I would be satisfied with what I have experienced.* There were 295.3 kilometers still to travel before we arrived in Santiago. However, I could not in that moment imagine them being any more significant or life giving than the kilometers we had just walked through the Meseta.

Two days after we parted—a day after my own experience at Cruz de Ferro—I received a message from

THE GOOD WAY

Rachel via Facebook. She told me how she had left a white stone at the base of the cross. Along with it, she also left a letter of forgiveness, releasing the person who had harmed her. In the process, her bonds were also cut loose. She was walking down from the highest point of the Camino, toward Santiago, unburdened and free.

Chapter Eleven

THE FALL

The days that followed our departure from Astorga seemed quieter. There were now only three of us starting out together each morning: Emilie, Allison, and myself. Sergio was walking at his own pace and would meet us each night at the albergue. He walked with us as far as Molinaseca, which was two days outside of Astorga. The place where we were staying was full by the time he arrived, so he found lodging just down the road. We had spent the early evening sitting by the river and enjoying one another's company. When it came time for dinner, I was not hungry and the ladies decided to grab something at the store. Sergio opted for a pilgrim's menu at a restaurant and promised to meet us back at our albergue. By the time he arrived, it was late, and Emilie and Allison had already headed up to bed. Sergio and I shared a few minutes of conversation, and then he headed off to his lodging for the night.

We did not know it at the time, but this was the last occasion we would be together on the Camino. He was on pace to arrive in Santiago a few days later than I would. If I'd recognized the significance of the moment, I would have told him what a blessing it had been to walk with him. I would have explained how much I had learned from the way he delighted in the journey and the things he was discovering along the way. I would have acknowledged the kindness I saw in him and the joy he brought to others. I would have called him brother, hugged him, and told him I would long for the day we could once again walk together. We would stay connected via the Internet as we walked separately. This gave me the opportunity to share with Sergio some of the ways he impacted me, but it was not the same as it would have been to be able to speak them to him face to face.

Emilie, Allison, and I were not alone. We were still walking with others, our Camino cousins, whom we had been keeping pace with for some time. While not as close as our immediate family, seeing them always brought a smile to our faces and gave us a sense we belonged to something bigger. When we arrived in a town, it would not feel like home for the night until we saw some of these people sitting at the restaurant along the road, already unpacking at the albergue, or walking in behind us later in the day.

With only three of us, there was more time on the trail to walk in silence and pray. We still began each morning walking together and would take a break to share a café con leche at some point, but for me the majority of these days were spent walking in an attitude of prayer. Right after we left Astorga, I talked to God about what had been happening during the past week and thanked Him for the gift of new family members. There was news from home, about friends who were experiencing loss, and my own family having to work through difficult circumstances. I could do nothing about these situations but pray. I would

The Fall

walk and hold them out to God. I would ask for what my friends and family needed. I also told Him about how powerless I felt and how I needed His help in trusting, waiting, and releasing. I spent time thanking God for all He had done in my life, for both the joyful and sorrowful times. Mostly, I would walk in silence, asking God to tell me whatever He desired. He gave me His presence more than words.

Our journey took us out of the Meseta and into the mountains of Galicia. The flat, dry landscape was being replaced with mountains, trees, and every shade of green you could imagine. We often walked along shaded paths or beside vineyards in full leaf. The price of all this beauty was steep climbs into the mountains and the descent down the other side. Walking for twenty-three days had strengthened our bodies for the challenge. While it was still strenuous, it did not tax us like our first days in the Pyrenees. One of the most significant climbs was still ahead of us. It would take us to O'Cebreiro, on a long day of walking 31.1 Kilometers. It would also be the last major climb of the Camino.

Our reward for making it to O'Cebreiro was a beautiful vista of the surrounding mountains. Others had decided to stop several kilometers below the summit to avoid the wind, which would often whip over the mountaintop, causing the nights to be chilly. We had pressed on and made it by midafternoon, enjoying the clear view under a blue sky dotted with puffy white clouds. Upon arriving in O'Cebreiro, we high-fived one another to celebrate completing what felt like the last big challenge of the Camino. The journey to Santiago seemed downhill from here. We settled into our albergue and headed out to explore the town, a beautifully restored medieval village.

THE GOOD WAY

Pilgrims and tourists intermingled while we visited the church and explored the shops. The clouds rolled in, the temperature dropped, and it started to drizzle. Our plans for taking in the sunset with a dinner of wine, cheese, and bread were thwarted. Instead, we would have dinner in the restaurant, turn in early, and begin the downward journey toward Santiago in the morning.

* * *

It was dark when we stepped out of the albergue. Beginning on a mountain ridge, rather than in the streets of a city, made it darker than most mornings. The first few minutes on the path left me wondering if we had gone the right way. We were walking on a narrow trail that led out of the village and into the woods. There were not many yellow arrows pointing the way, and it was hard to see where we were walking. I might have assumed we had gone the wrong way except for a couple of other pilgrims ahead of us. If we were lost, at least we would not be alone.

It took us about three kilometers before we hit a spot on the trail that turned right onto a forest road. This was clearly marked and removed any uncertainty about where we were headed. We were now walking on a wide road covered with crushed stone. With the sun finally rising, we saw dawn breaking over the surrounding mountains. The sky was clear, and the oranges and reds of the advancing sun chased away the last vestiges of night. The three of us were walking together, enjoying the morning and savoring the beauty displayed before us.

By the time we approached the next village, the morning was in full bloom. We were still on a wide path

The Fall

covered with small stones. As we turned a corner, allowing the village to come into view, I could see a large group of people standing around. It was as if a tour bus had just dropped them off to begin their Camino journey. I was distracted by the commotion they were making, not watching where I was placing my feet. I must have stepped on a small rock, because just then my ankle gave out and I fell to my knees. Emilie and Allison came to help me up and see if I was all right. Though my knees were scraped, I was more embarrassed than injured. Earlier in the day, falling might have been expected, since we walked in the dark over uneven forest paths. But here the road was wide and gravel-covered—not difficult. I got up, dusted myself off, tested my ankle, and began walking again.

Not a hundred yards down the path, I was once again preoccupied by the group at the edge of town and turned my ankle a second time. Now doubly embarrassed, I tried to get up quickly and act as if it were no big deal. Thankfully, my ankle still felt okay, and I continued walking. As I did, I thought, *Third time is a charm.* I had better be careful the rest of the day—the steep section was yet to come, and I did not know how many more twists my ankle could take.

Soon we were in the midst of the big group. They were happy to be there and enjoyed one another's company so much they were constantly calling to each other, laughing, and even singing. These were good things, unless you were looking forward to walking in silence and prayer. I tried to get ahead of them, but some were too quick. I stopped to let them pass, walking again only when there was ample distance between us. This only provided momentary relief. Not long after they passed me, someone in their group would stop to rest or adjust something. They would begin walking again only after I had caught back up. It went on like this for nine kilometers.

By the time we reached Alto do Polo, our first opportunity for café con leche, I had finally passed by them. Emilie and Allison were still caught in their throng. I ordered our usual and waited for my companions. By the time they arrived, the large group was already filling up the place. It was fun to have so much energy at the restaurant; I just desired a little less of it on the trail. To allow them their revelry and allow for our desired solitude, we departed quicker than usual.

I would walk the next twelve kilometers mostly alone. The journey down the mountain was beautiful, though often steep. The space gave me time to think about what God had been doing in me over the past twenty-six days. It also gave me the ability to concentrate fully on where I was placing each step. The steepest section of the day would come right before we arrived in Triacastela, and I did not want to be distracted.

Despite my concentrated efforts, it was on this steep section that I took my third spill of the day. Unlike the wide road we walked on earlier, this was a mountain trail that had ruts carved from rainwater. In spots, the dirt was transformed into slippery mud from recent rains. Stones of all sizes covered the path.

Focusing on the path ahead, I heard footsteps closing in on me. I veered off to the side to let the person pass. Just as he came alongside of me, my right foot hit a fist-sized stone. My ankle buckled, but unlike earlier in the day, the path was not wide or flat enough to fall relatively safely. I did not want to lunge at the man who was now beside me, so I attempted to steady myself on my walking pole and

The Fall

my left foot. But the pole bent, and my left foot hit another large rock and twisted. It was a twofer—two twisted ankles in one fall.

I went down hard. The people passing me immediately grabbed my arms and got me back to my feet. They did not speak any English and simply conveyed their hope I was okay with a smile and nod. My right ankle felt fine, but my left ankle definitely didn't. When I put weight on it, I felt shooting pain. I hobbled for a couple of steps and nodded my head back at those who had stopped. Seeing I was upright, they turned and walked on.

With another two kilometers till our next stop, I hobbled for half a kilometer before I found a place to sit down and remove my shoe. Just then, Emilie and Allison arrived. Once they understood what had happened and how badly I had twisted my ankle, they went into action. Both of them removed items from my pack to lighten it and loaded them into their own. We talked about whether we should get a taxi or if I should keep walking. Before we could make a decision, some people we had seen for most of our journey also arrived. One took off a compression strap he had around his knee and wrapped my ankle. Another picked up my pack and started for Triacastela. Allison would go ahead with them to secure a place in the albergue. Emilie would walk with me. It felt like a whirlwind, but in the span of just a few moments, all these people mobilized to help me. I felt the pain of my injury, but I also felt very loved.

Emilie and I began to walk slowly toward the village. We talked about what we would do once we got there. I knew I would need to ice my ankle. I also knew I would need to find some kind of brace or compression strap. Walking with Emilie was comforting. This was our twenty-sixth day of walking together, and I did not want it to be our last. I had been saving a rest day and now I was pretty sure I was going to need it. I did not know if I would have to stop for a day or if I would be able to walk a much shorter distance in the morning, breaking the next day's journey into two. Either way, Emilie and I would part company sooner than expected. Thankfully, those decisions would have to wait. Right now all I could focus on was covering the next 1.5 kilometers.

Halfway there, one of the women in the group who had stopped ran back. She said she was a runner and this was not hard for her. She wanted Emilie's pack and would put it in the queue to hold a spot for her at the albergue. Emilie handed over the pack and continued to walk with me. The longer we walked, the more it was sinking in—this might be the last distance I covered on the Camino. Emilie must have sensed what was going through my mind, because she tried to encourage me and kept the conversation light.

Sooner than I could have imagined, we made our way into town and toward the line of people in front of the albergue. Emilie and Allison went into town to purchase food for lunch and to see what they could find at the pharmacy to help my ankle. By the time they returned, we still had about a half hour before the albergue opened. We spread out our lunch and ate. The balance of the afternoon was spent applying ice to my swollen ankle. I took ibuprofen at the maximum allowable doses and massaged my leg with arnica cream in between each icing. I was doing all I knew to do to help my ankle heal quickly.

Half a day earlier, I had been thinking it was all downhill to Santiago. Now, it felt as if I had another mountain to climb. When I massaged the outside of my left

The Fall

ankle, I could feel a clicking. I did not know if something was broken, torn, or just out of place. The next day, I would read on the Internet that with a severe sprain a tendon can come out of the groove it normally rests in and make this sound. But when I headed off to bed, I had no idea what was wrong. All I could do was turn to God in prayer, asking for healing, but with a willingness to yield. I cried out, *You know what I desire, Lord. I want to continue this journey, but you know best. Not my will, but your will be done.*

Five days earlier, I had walked out of Astorga thinking that if my Camino ended there, I would be satisfied. Now the real possibility of it being over was staring me in the face, I did not feel the same contentment. While I sat outside with ice on my ankle, people I had been keeping pace with stopped to ask what happened and how was I feeling. As I explained, they would wince and say how sorry they were. While they wished me well, I could see it in their eyes—they did not think I would be going any farther. Oh, how I prayed they were wrong.

The next morning, we got up as usual. Putting on my left shoe was difficult, with my foot being wrapped tightly in the compression straps Emilie and Allison had found at the pharmacy. I felt shooting pain when I maneuvered my ankle into the shoe. Within a half hour of getting up, we made our way to the bar across the field. A path was cut through the grass that had been worn down by pilgrims and eroded by rain. Several times in the short distance, my foot twisted as I placed it down on the uneven ground. Before I crossed the field, I knew I would not be walking any farther that day. The bar had not yet opened. We sat at a table outside, and I told Emilie and Allison I did not think I could continue. It seemed to me I had two choices—stay here another night or take a taxi to the next

THE GOOD WAY

town, Sarria, which was larger. There, I would have access to care if I needed it and the ability to catch a bus or train if I could not go on. I told the ladies I would take a taxi to Sarria, rest up, and then hopefully be able to walk again in two days.

With sadness, Emilie said she could not stay with me. Her family was meeting her in Santiago on the 29th. She could not get there in time if she waited two days. I gave her my blessing to move on, and Allison too. After all, I could not guarantee I would be able to walk in two days. There was a good chance I would have to take a bus to Santiago. If so, I told them I would meet them in the square. We might just see each other again.

The bar opened, and we decided to have one last café con leche together. Emilie spoke to the barista about calling a taxi. He told us there would be a bus at 7:20 and where to catch it. This was not exactly how I had imagined our last café con leche together. It was hard to engage in chitchat and even harder to share what was really going on internally. Not because I did not trust them, but because I did not want to make them feel any worse than they already did.

* * *

They walked in front of me, carrying my pack between them, as we made our way to the bus stop. With a half hour before the bus arrived, the ladies asked if I wanted them to wait. I said no. There was no reason for them to delay starting out any longer, and saying goodbye would just get harder. They situated my pack, we gave each other hugs, and then they walked on. We all had known there would be a day in the near future when we would have to

The Fall

say goodbye. We just did not think it would come so quickly or under these circumstances. I felt lonely as I watched them walk away. I now felt completely alone on the Camino, more alone than when I arrived in St. Jean. Watching them go also took me to another place and tapped into something much deeper.

When I began this journey, I had hoped it would be a physical manifestation of the internal journey I'd been on for the previous two years. While I walked, I had been walking back through betrayal, hurt, loss, and forgiveness. God had also been gracious enough to allow me to experience created space where new family entered in. In this way, He was giving me a glimpse of what rebirth and resurrection might look like in the future. While I could not yet fully see it in my life back at home, my life on the Camino had brought me hope. Now, as I was standing there, watching the last two members of my Camino family walk away, this journey was taking me to the one place I did not want to return.

After I was let go from my church, people asked me what it felt like. I would describe my feelings and what it was like to have it done in such an unkind manner. It had felt like being on a bus that slowed down long enough to open its doors and toss me to the curb. It felt as if I were no longer wanted, valued, or loved. I had been thrown from the only community I had known as a pastor. In the process, I received severe cuts, scrapes, and bruises from the impact. It felt as if I was in the gutter, writhing in pain, and the bus closed its doors and pulled away. Doubled over, I watched the bus continue down the road, getting smaller and smaller as it drove on toward the next town, where it would pick up new passengers.

I wanted desperately to get up from the gutter. I

longed for the cuts, scrapes, and bruises to be healed. I would do anything to move on, but each time I tried to stand I would hear God tell me to wait. But I am better at pressing on than waiting. I am more inclined to move quickly than to walk slowly. By the time I had been let go, the senior pastor had been out of work for eight months. People were beginning to whisper about what was taking him so long to find a position. What no one took into account was how much he needed to heal.

Right after I was let go, a mentor said to me assuredly, "Ron, I do not see you being out of work for eight months. You are the kind of guy who will find something quickly." I was encouraged by his confidence. Neither he, nor I, took into account that God might be up to something far more significant. I never imagined that fourteen months later, I would still be without a clear vision of where God was leading me, or that I would be standing on the side of the road in Triacastela, bruised and injured, waiting for a bus.

Chapter Twelve

COMPASSION AND COMFORT

Walking from the bus station to where the Camino makes its way through the town of Sarria was difficult, but I did not have to do it alone. As I waited for the bus in Triacastela, another American came and stood by the curb. He understood getting on the bus meant something was wrong and asked me what had happened. I explained my plight and what my immediate plans were. He had injured his foot early on and had been taking the bus through many sections of the Camino as his wife continued walking. He told me about how long it took before he could walk again and the struggle he was still having. He had nursed his injury for the majority of the way and was now hoping, with only five days left, to walk the final 115 kilometers to Santiago. I did not have the kind of time he had taken to recuperate and his story was not instilling a great deal of hope in me. His presence, however, was a gift. He knew, as well as anyone could, what I was feeling.

More than his story, what he shared with me was compassion and kindness. When we arrived in Sarria, he went into the bus station to grab maps for both of us. The building was not far from where we had been dropped off, but at this point any additional walking was painful. His willingness to do this little errand was helpful. After we oriented ourselves on the map, I selected the shortest path to the Camino. He asked if I minded if he walked with me—I was grateful for the company. As we made our way to the albergue, we talked about life and faith. I limped along slowly, but he was patient with my pace.

When we reached the street where the Camino makes its way through town, he told me he had to go find the hotel where he and his wife would be staying for the night. I thanked him for seeing me this far and expressed my gratitude for his company. He wished me well and walked on.

I found the albergue where I thought I might stay and was pleased to discover their Wi-Fi signal extended to the street and did not require an access code. It was just after eight o'clock in the morning in Spain, meaning it was 11:00 p.m. back at home. I began messaging Tammie to let her know I had arrived and what I planned to do for the next two days as I rested. I realized as I typed that I had no control over whether I would be able to continue. The last twenty-one hours had been about icing and stabilizing my ankle and getting to a place where I could recuperate. Sitting against the wall with my leg propped up on my backpack, emotions washed over me. I was typing on my smart phone and tears flowed down my face. Sobs began to well up inside me, and I felt like I would start bawling at any moment.

Tammie texted me the question, "What is driving most of the emotion?" It was not knowing if I would be able to finish the Camino and the feelings this exposed regarding my inability to finish out my calling at the church and not knowing what was next regarding my vocation. It all felt

Compassion and Comfort

jumbled. I texted back, "It is sitting here in the not knowing." She asked, "What is it to walk in the good way right here?" I responded, "To trust, even when what comes next is unclear." Despite what I was feeling, and with the help of my wife's questions, I knew I would choose to trust.

Just then, a woman stopped on the street in front of me and asked if I was okay. I lied and said yes, but also briefly told her about my twisted ankle and what I was hoping the next forty-eight hours would hold. I had not seen this woman on the trail before, so it was a great act of kindness when she asked if there was anything she could do for me. I knew she would try to meet any need I might express, but there was really nothing to do. I told her I would be all right—I was just waiting for the albergue to open, but I appreciated her stopping. The compassion on her face made her, in the moment, one of the most beautiful people I had met.

Early on in the transition from our church, a passage from 2 Corinthians helped me to gain perspective as I was suffering the pain and loss of being removed: "Praise be to the God and Father of our Lord Jesus Christ, the Father of compassion and the God of all comfort, who comforts us in all our troubles, so that we can comfort those in any trouble with the comfort we ourselves receive from God" (1:3-4). The brief and unexpected encounter with this woman felt like a tangible expression of God's compassion and comfort.

When she realized there was nothing more she could offer, she smiled, told me she would send good wishes my way, and walked on. She was like an angel, a being that acts as an intermediary from God. I knew she was a fellow pilgrim, but that did not prevent her from also being a messenger from God. I was experiencing what it was to have the Father of compassion and comfort care for me in my time of trouble.

The night before I left for Spain, I had asked some people who had gathered to send me off to pray for humility, compassion, and a servant's heart as I sought to be the presence of Christ to others. I also asked them to pray that I might see the presence of Christ in those I would meet. It was less than two hours after Emilie and Allison were forced to leave me behind, and the first two people I met had been the presence of Christ to me. The prayers of my friends back at home had been answered all along the Camino, but on this morning they seemed to be particularly powerful and effective.

This experience of kindness and compassion provided me with enough hope to get me off the pavement and down to the next corner, where I found a bar owner willing to fill my Ziploc bag with ice and allow me to occupy a table for as long as I like. I sat there for the next hour and a half, alternating between icing my ankle and massaging it with arnica cream. The owner seemed especially kind as he did whatever he could to help. Over the next two days, every time I would make my way to his establishment, he greeted me with a smile and often offered to fill my bag with ice before I asked. We did not speak the same language, but I understood his compassion toward me quite clearly.

By midmorning, the first pilgrims who had started their morning somewhere between Triacastela and Sarria walked past where I sat on the Camino. Many were people I had met as I walked. The ones I knew stopped to ask what had happened and then expressed hope I would be able to continue. Some had already heard the news I had

Compassion and Comfort

been injured and said they had been praying for me. As we talked, I could sense that my situation produced some internal conflict in them. They were genuinely concerned but did not know what to say or how to help. This was a reaction I was familiar with.

Having stayed in the same city where I served as a pastor, I would run into people who attended my former church. They would ask me how I was and what I was doing. I would answer, "I'm good, but God has us waiting. I am not sure what is next." They would often get the same look I now saw on the face of my fellow pilgrims. They were also unsure what they should say or how they could help. This can feel uncomfortable because most of us are not as adept at simply being *with* others as we are at doing something *to* or *for* them. Like the people back home, my fellow pilgrims could not do anything *to* or *for* me, and since they were passing through they did not have the time to be *with* me but for a moment.

With each person who stopped and then walked on, I realized I might not see them again. I was grateful for the opportunity to connect with them. Knowing they genuinely cared was comforting. Watching them move on, however, was hard. My heart desired to go and be with them. I would remain in a place of waiting while they kept moving. While this quite possibly would be the last time I would see any of the people who were kind enough to stop, I dared not bring this up while they were standing in front of me. I did not want to pronounce the death of my hopes of making it to Santiago on my own two feet before it was absolutely clear my journey was done. Instead, I would wish the travelers well and simply say we will see what tomorrow holds. Many offered to pray for me. I thanked them and said I would love it if they did.

THE GOOD WAY

I found an albergue that would let me check in early. I also arranged to stay there two nights so I could heal. The woman who ran the place was very kind. Long before it was open, she let me select a bed, take a shower, and make myself at home. I was trying to figure out what my options were. Since neither of us spoke each other's language, I used Google Translate to communicate my questions. Understanding her responses was not as easy, but with a bit of pointing and some big smiles, we were able to make do.

After I got settled and rested for a while, I made my way back to the street. There was a chance Emilie and Allison would be walking through the town soon, and I wanted to let them know I was settled. I never saw them, but others I knew began to come into town. Many were surprised to see me. After we updated one another on the last day or two, they would ask me where I was staying and then go and reserve a bed for themselves at the same place.

By lunchtime, I welcomed Jonathan and Andrew, a father and son who had walked portions of the Camino over the past four years and would complete it in just a few days. I first met them at the albergue where I had been introduced to the Kiwis. Jonathan and Andrew had shared many accommodations and some meals with us along the way. They checked into the albergue and then came back to share a meal with me. How gracious God was to not allow me to eat alone. After all the shared meals over the past twenty-seven days, eating alone seemed like one of the loneliest experiences I could imagine.

A little while later, I saw Jay and his wife, Deb, a friendly couple from Arizona who were always willing to share the knowledge they gained from walking the

Compassion and Comfort

Camino years earlier. They had stayed in this albergue on their last pilgrimage and had decided to return. While on the bus, I had picked out another place to stay. Only because of the kindness of the woman who ran this one did I end up here. As I listened to Jay tell why they had chosen to sleep here for the night, I recognized how gracious God was being to me. Earlier in the day, I had stood waiting for the bus, thinking I was alone. I was now seeing how circumstances were working together to place me with people I knew. I might be alone in the days ahead, but today I was among friends.

Jay and Deb had heard I was injured and were happy to see me. News travels fast on the Camino, even faster with access to the Internet. I told them what had happened and what my plans were. I was thinking of walking to the next village in the morning, since it was only three kilometers away. I thought this would allow me to ease back into walking and break a normal day's trek into two shorter ones. Jay listened to my reasoning and then recommended I stay put. "Everything you need is right outside the door," he said, adding, "The next town is far smaller and would be less conducive to resting. Another day of rest would do you good." I explained exactly what my ankle felt like and told him of the "clicking" I had felt the night before. Jay had experienced severe sprains before, and I could tell by his expression that he was not convinced I would continue. "It would be easier to catch a bus or train from Sarria than it would from the next town," he offered. I knew for certain he doubted I would walk to Santiago.

By late afternoon, it seemed as if half the albergue was filled with people I had met on the journey. Two men from Japan who had stopped to help me along the trail when I fell were here, and with them a couple of others who had been keeping pace with us. I had a feeling it would not be like this tomorrow. The wave of people I had been walking with would have moved through. I tried not to think about it. Instead, I was simply grateful they were here.

Less than half a day earlier, I had stood at a curb, feeling alone and abandoned. I had cried out to God, "I do not know how much more I can take." Apparently, He understood how desperate I felt. He heard my cry, and in His grace He responded to my plea.

Having seen such tangible expressions of God's compassion throughout the day, a person might be tempted to feel shame over having cried out in desperation in the first place. I felt none of it. In the months prior to leaving for Spain, I walked a lot, covering hundreds of kilometers in preparation for the Camino. I had been engaging even longer in exercising the ability to bring my heart to God, no matter its condition. While Hartwell Park was my training ground for walking, the book of Psalms was the training ground for my heart. More than half of the Psalms were written by David who, Scripture tells us, was a man after God's own heart. David had no problem coming to God with the truth of his heart. He cried out:

"I call on the Lord in my distress" (Psalm 12:1).

"Out of the depth I cry to you, O Lord" (Psalm 130:1).

"My bones are in agony. My soul is in anguish. How long, O Lord, how long?" (Psalm 6:3).

If it is appropriate for David to cry out to God in his distress, it is appropriate for us as well. This cry is in no way a condemnation of God. He is not put off or threatened by it. This is not a matter of saying, "God, you are not powerful, kind, and compassionate enough to rescue me." In fact, our cry of distress is an acknowledgment that God alone is capable of meeting us in our deepest need. It is also an admission we cannot save ourselves. We are powerless over our circumstances and even ourselves. While we still believe we can control and affect the outcome, we have no reason to call out to God. We walk in our self-sufficiency. Rather than being fully dependent on Him, we handle it on our own. This isolates us from the ability to recognize His compassion and comfort.

Frequently, we recognize God's kindness to us only after the fact. That's because in the present moment, we are too busy trying to orchestrate the outcome in our own strength. How often have we not recognized God's compassion and care because we were too focused on formulating our own plan? In order to fully see God and His working in my life, I have to take my eyes off myself and my circumstances. Sometimes the only way I can get to this place is to come to the end of my strength and efforts. In my distress, I cry out to Him, and He answers me.

When David was about fifteen years old, his father sent him to take supplies to his brothers at the battlefield where the armies of Israel faced off against the Philistines. It must have been an exciting journey for a boy who spent most of his time in the fields tending sheep. When David arrived, he quickly dropped off the supplies and went to the frontlines to see what was happening. In the process, he heard Goliath step out from the Philistine line and taunt the armies of Israel. The men of Israel fled in fear—all except David. While the others backed away, David volunteered to fight this giant of a man. He had no armor, nor any military training that we know about. All he had was a sling, a few smooth stones, and the confidence that

THE GOOD WAY

Almighty God intervenes for those who lack their own might. He said, "The Lord who rescued me from the paw of the lion and the paw of the bear will rescue me from the hand of this Philistine" (1 Samuel 17:37). David knew what it was to call out to God when the circumstances were overwhelming and he was not sufficient to handle them. In the process, he discovered God to be fully capable and deeply concerned about what David was facing.

Each cry of distress by David is accompanied by an affirmation of God's ability to rescue and David's willingness to trust. David also cried out, "The Lord is my light and my salvation – whom shall I fear? The Lord is the stronghold of my life – of whom shall I be afraid?" (Psalm 27:11). Many of David's psalms begin and end with a declaration of who God is and David's trust in Him. Sandwiched in between are pleas for help or a pouring out of the psalmist's heart.

As I went through my day, returning over and over again to prayer, I tried to remember this rhythm. I would affirm who God is and what He is to me. I would declare my trust in Him, and then I would feel the freedom to share all that was on my heart. I still felt fear, anxiety, helplessness, and disappointment. I would bring these things to God, because I knew I could not handle them on my own. I knew He was, and would be, my light and salvation. This gave me confidence, no matter what the next day would hold. I would also share gratitude and thanksgiving for all the little ways I had seen Him demonstrate His compassion and care throughout the day. I could echo the song of David in 2 Samuel 22:7: "In my distress I called to the Lord; I called out to my God. From his temple he heard my voice; my cry came to his ears."

Despite watching Emilie and Allison walk away in the

morning and still not knowing if I could continue on, it had been a good day, a day filled with big and small expressions of God's compassion and comfort. I still had no control over whether I would recover enough to walk any farther. I had no idea what tomorrow would be like once all the people at the albergue moved on. I did, however, have confidence in the one to whom I could cry out.

Even so, I went to bed wondering what the morning would hold. Would I feel better or would hours of not massaging and icing my ankle cause it to stiffen up? Only time and a night's rest would tell. I put in my ear buds, turned on my iPod, and listened to music that declared the power of God. I then drifted off to sleep in the tension between my desire to continue on toward Santiago and my willingness to trust God with whatever the morning brought.

Chapter Thirteen

LAVISH LOVE

I fumbled around for my iPod so I could check the time. It was 5:30 a.m. Normally, I would have slipped out of bed, grabbed my pack and sleeping bag, and quietly made my way to the common area so I could go through my morning ritual before heading out. I would not be walking today. There was no reason to risk waking the others, so I just lay there thinking about where I found myself on this journey.

When I had spoken to Tammie the day before, she reminded me I had desired my experience on the Camino to be a physical manifestation of the internal spiritual-emotional journey I had been on for the past two years. She said it did not surprise her I had been hurt. This trauma to my ankle seemed to her a mirror of the trauma I had experienced. She almost had a bit of joy in her voice as she asked me a question just before we concluded our Skype session. "What do you think God is up to in all of this?" The only answer I could give her in the moment was, "I am not completely sure, but I am listening and hoping to find out."

As I lay there, I thought about what had transpired

since I had twisted my ankle on the final descent. I thought of the people who came to my rescue and the care Emilie and Allison had shown me. I thought about the compassion and comfort God had demonstrated to me through people, many of whom were still sleeping in the bunks that surrounded me. I also thought about what the next twenty-four hours would bring. I stretched both of my ankles to compare how they felt. It did not take me but a second to feel the sharp pain shoot up my leg as I tried to rotate my left ankle. I did not receive a miraculous healing over night. I knew my day would be filled with icing, massaging, and ibuprofen. I also knew I would try a little walking. I thought I would have to loosen up the ankle if I was going to walk any distance the next day.

As people began to stir, I realized it would not be long before they all moved on. I did not want to think about what it would feel like to watch them leave. What was God up to in all of this?

* * *

When I first left the church, there was a hand full of people who rallied around us. They told us how much they loved us and offered to help in any way. These interactions were vitally important in the beginning stages of processing the loss and grief. It was helpful to see compassion and comfort in the eyes of those we had walked with for so long. They also told us they knew God was about to do something in our lives and were excited to see what it was. They would speak this with such conviction that it made us believe too, even when it was hard to discern what God was doing.

There were also those we had lived so much life with

who simply went silent. I think many simply did not know what to say. They may have even been shell shocked by the amount of transition the church family had experienced in the previous year. The fact we were no longer part of the regular rhythm of their lives allowed the relationships to simply slip away.

When we were part of the same local body of believers, it was as if we were all sitting in individual inner tubes on the open ocean. Because we were a family, we linked our arms and legs together so our inner tubes stayed together. As the swells passed under us, we would rise and dip with the rolling energy of the ocean. Because we were linked together, the movement did not cause us to pull apart. Being separated from our church felt like our arms and legs were no longer intertwined. In the beginning, this did not seem to make much of a difference. We were all still floating in close proximity to one another. It was still relatively easy to support, encourage, and love one another. Over time, however, the rolling energy of the ocean began to create distance between us. We began to drift apart.

This was not intentional. No one was paddling away. Time and the swells of life slowly moved us away from one another. In the midst of it, we did not notice the power and consistency of the rolling tide, but at some point we looked around to discover even the closest inner tubes were some distance away. This realization produced feelings of loneliness and isolation.

* * *

The inner-tube imagery returned to my mind when people finally started to climb from their bunks and prepare to leave the albergue. It felt like the rising and falling of the ocean. It felt as if the drift would begin.

I got up with them and moved into my normal morning routine. I would not be walking today, but I could not bring myself to lie there as they all left. I had arranged to stay in the albergue for an extra night, but I did not know if I would have to vacate while it was cleaned, so I packed up my gear as I had done for each of the last twenty-nine days. It was a weird feeling to get ready, knowing I wasn't going anywhere. About the time I finished, people began to depart. Those I knew said goodbye and wished me the best. I told them I hoped to see them in Santiago in a few days. As each one departed, it felt as if another swell was passing underneath me. I was drifting away from my Camino family just a little more.

By the time they were all gone, I felt down. I was alone once again and could not imagine I would have the same experience I'd had the day before. Most of the people we had been walking with had passed through. The people we had walked away from in Astorga were more than a day behind me, and I had no hope of them catching up to me. I prepared myself emotionally for a day of simply sitting with the question Tammie had asked: "What was God doing in all of this?"

The albergue had free Wi-Fi, but the signal was not strong enough to cover the sleeping area. Now that everyone had departed, I moved to the common area to pick up a signal. I wanted to see if I had any messages from the people at home who had been following my journey and who were faithfully praying for me. Since my injury, they had provided as much compassion and comfort as the people who were present with me on the Camino. When I opened up Facebook, I had a notification telling me Helen had made a comment on my post telling people about my injury and asking for prayer. She simply said, "We are coming, Ron! Can't wait to see you tonight!"

Immediately, my eyes filled with tears. I knew what it would cost them to get to me, since they were a day and a half behind. It would be a long, hard day of walking, and yet they were coming. Helen, Rachel, Amy, and Rolando would arrive by late afternoon. I had been feeling down and imagined myself spending the day opening my heart to what God was teaching me about relationships that drift apart. God was doing something else. I was now filled with excitement about the arrival of my family. It felt as if they were on a rescue mission. In their willingness to not allow the inner tubes to separate—and instead to paddle back together—I felt deeply loved.

Sitting there in gratitude, I knew what I would do with the day. I would do everything possible to be physically ready to walk together in the morning. Knowing how little control I had over this, I would call out to God for help. And I would also ensure they had a place to stay when they got here.

The Camino has gotten very busy in the past few years. Karen told me of her first experiences. People would walk at a leisurely pace, choosing conversation over speed. If they arrived in a town at five or six o'clock in the evening, they would still find a bed. This is no longer true. There were places where people would arrive in the early afternoon and find all the albergues full. On more than one occasion, I watched people arrive into town, tired from a long day of walking. Their faces were filled with relief, because they thought they were done for the day. To their dismay, they would discover all lodging for the night was full, forcing them to continue to the next village. I did not want this to happen to my family. I used Google Translate to communicate with the woman who was running the albergue. She was kind enough to allow me to pay in advance for their overnight stay and reserve beds for them. They might arrive tired, but at least they could be confident they would have a place to sleep.

Now that accommodations were arranged, I went to work on rehabilitating my ankle. I would take a walk from the albergue to the church, a few meters back up the Camino. My ankle was stiff and sore, but if I wrapped it tightly it felt like I could walk without causing further injury. After my short lap, I would massage it for thirty minutes and then apply ice for another half hour. I repeated the process throughout the morning. While I could not walk without a significant limp, the ankle definitely felt better than yesterday. I thought, *If tomorrow brings the same amount of progress, I think I will be walking.*

In my fall, I collapsed one of my walking poles and bent the other. I wanted to get something more trustworthy. On one of my trips to the church, I gingerly made my way down a huge set of stairs to a shop situated at the bottom. It had a rack of walking sticks outside its door. I was able to select one that seemed to be the right height and felt good in my hand. I leaned hard on it and found it to be more than capable of supporting my weight. I was happy to have found such a suitable companion. More importantly, I was able to get up and down those stairs. This made me feel as if I might have a chance of handling the Camino's inclines and descents sure to come.

My prayers were turning from calls for help to expressions of thankfulness.

By late morning, I was on the third rotation of my regime, sitting at a street-side table at the cafe next to the albergue with my foot elevated and wrapped in ice. I was writing postcards to make the most of the time. When I finished penning one, I looked up and saw Father Stephen and his nephew. I cannot remember the first time we stopped at the same village, but Father Stephen had been walking in rhythm with us for much of the Camino. Some days back, they had decided to stop to rest before the climb into O'Cebreiro while our group had continued on. It had put them a day behind us, and now they were catching up. He was traveling with a group from Philadelphia that was staying in the monastery for the night. He and his nephew asked where I was lodging. I told them about the albergue and the kindness of the lady who ran it. The two of them decided to bunk with me. My second night in Sarria, and I would once again be surrounded by people I'd been walking with.

For the next few hours, we sat at the table as the group from Philadelphia slowly trickled into town. Rather than simply spending an afternoon waiting around, it was filled with good conversation, laughter, and a great sense of blessing.

The Kiwis had sent a message to me along the way, saying they would arrive around 3:30. It was then that I started looking down the street, anticipating I would see them at any moment. But there was no sign of them. By 4:15, I could not take it any longer and I made my way back down the street to the top of the stairs. I knew they would have to climb them to get to the albergue. As I sat there, I thought of how gracious it was for them to press on through the long day so they could see how I was doing.

Helen was the first to round the corner. She had a smile on her face, and her eyes lit up as soon as she saw me. Her smile got even bigger as she climbed the stairs. Mine widened as well. Joy was breaking out all over the place. When she reached the top, we hugged and I told her how thankful I was they had come. After a minute of standing in gratitude, she told me the others were a bit farther behind. Helen had been the one who suffered with knee pain early on and because of it had often been in the rear of the group. In the week since I had walked away from them in Astorga, she had become a trailblazer. She had grown so much on the Camino: mentally, emotionally, spiritually, and physically. You could tell by the look on her face that her soul was doing well.

We decided to drop off Helen's pack at the albergue, and then she would head back to see if she could carry anything for the others to help them with the final push into town. She was tired from a long day of walking, but I struggled to keep up with her as we headed back up the street. Once the pack was dropped off, she went back down the street. I waited a few minutes, but the anticipation was getting the best of me so I headed back down to the top of the stairs to wait. The whole group bypassed the stairs and took a side street and came back to the Camino behind me. They were almost at the albergue before I could catch them. When I did, we all embraced, and I told them what a huge gift it was for them to come. It felt as if our inner tubes were once again floating together and our arms were intertwined.

Almost immediately, they began to tell about their experiences and the people they had met since the last time we were together. They asked how I had been injured and how the ankle was doing now. They asked how it felt to have Emilie leave and what the last two days had been like. I was able to tell them how compassionate God had been and about all the people He brought to me. I also told them I was treating for dinner; we were going to celebrate our reunion.

By 7:30, we were sitting outside the bar owned by the fellow who supplied me with ice for the past two days. When we told him we were going to order dinner, he brought out a tablecloth to cover the plastic table. It seemed a fitting upgrade for the occasion. We were joined by Thomas, a friend they had made over the past few days. He was from France, and when we were introduced, he said to me, "You know, we French do not have a very high opinion of Americans." Everyone around the table tensed. I replied, "That's okay. We Americans do not have a very high opinion of the French either." We both laughed.

When the wine was brought to the table, we lifted our glasses and toasted one another. Dinner seemed to taste exceptionally good, no doubt enhanced by the company. We talked, laughed, and lingered for quite a while, but it was getting late and the four of them had come a very long way. They were tired and ready to turn in, so we made our way back to the albergue. It could not have been a better day.

Back at the albergue, I was preparing to massage my ankle one last time before bed. Helen came over and asked if she could do it. I told her walking so far in one day to catch up with me was gift enough. I knew how tired she was, but she insisted. She said she not only wanted to massage it, but she also wanted to pray over it. I gave up the protest and handed her my arnica cream. Helen knelt at my feet and began to rub the cream onto my ankle. As she massaged the area, she stopped every so often and held her hands over the injury. I knew she was praying when she did this. She would then begin massaging the ankle again, until she once again felt prompted by the Holy Spirit to pray. I let go of any hesitation I might have experienced about letting Helen do this and simply allowed myself to be present with God in the moment. When she finished, she kissed the injury, handed me the tube of cream, and said, "Massage is helpful, but it is the prayer that is really effective." All I could say was, "Thank you for both."

It felt like a lavish act of love. I wondered if this is how Jesus had felt when the women came and anointed his feet while he was having dinner with Simon the Pharisee. Jesus' host had ignored the customs of the day and did not provide Him with a kiss of greeting, water to wash His feet, or oil to anoint His head. The woman at his feet could not stop kissing them. She washed them with her tears of gratitude, dried them with her hair, and anointed them with perfume. Helen anointed me with her presence and prayer. While I would not say arnica cream smells like perfume, the "fragrance" from this act of love was just as sweet. I knew Helen was grateful that God had brought us together on the Camino and for the words of encouragement He had spoken to her through me. This seemed to be her way of demonstrating gratitude.

If I had some understanding of what Jesus may have experienced, I had even more connection to what the leper must have felt to have the Lord touch and heal him. Lepers were unclean, and their uncleanliness spread to those who touched them. Because of this, people avoided them. For the last two days, people were kind to me, but I also had the sense—silly as it sounds—that they did not want to get too close for fear they might catch whatever bad luck had befallen me. Usually, I felt this with the acquaintances I would run into and not so much from my Camino family.

Lavish Love

Still, I knew that what I had, nobody else wanted.

* * *

It had felt like that back at home as well. We consistently felt God was calling us to wait. Just when we would think the waiting was over, once again through Scripture, circumstances, or someone in our life, God would speak the word *wait*. It sounds so good on paper. "Wait for the Lord; be strong and take heart and wait for the Lord" (Psalm 27:14). And, "Those who wait for the Lord will gain new strength" (Isaiah 40:31). As the waiting extended past several months and into a year, people got a look in their eyes that seemed to say, "I don't want what you have got."

Even deeper than this is the feeling that comes when you are tossed off the bus, when you are told we do not need the gifts God has given you anymore. You feel as if you have become an untouchable. You know this is wrong thinking. You ask for God to help you cover over the lie with the truth of who He declares you to be. But it takes time to heal this wound and walk in the truth. It also takes the ability to see the truth in someone else's eyes. This is the power of healing that can only be found in relationship with others.

I wonder how much was healed in the leper's heart when Jesus touched his skin. It was probably the first time in years he had felt the touch of another human being. When Jesus touched him, the leper knew what it felt like for someone to bestow value and worth on him. He knew what it was to be treated as clean and loved.

That is what it felt like Helen bestowed upon me, with the laying on of her hands. The morning would tell us if

Helen's massage and prayer were effective in preparing my ankle to walk again, but they had already done powerful healing work in my heart.

I settled into my bunk and began talking to God about the lavish love I had just experienced. A couple of weeks earlier, I had spoken words to Helen that I believed the Holy Spirit had wanted me to share. At the time, I knew it was a God-ordained moment. Now, I was wondering who it was intended for. For the past few weeks, I had thought it had been for Helen—now I was not so sure.

Maybe I was the one God had ordained to be healed through our meeting on the Camino. Then again, our God is so creative that He could have orchestrated events for both of us to be healed as we encountered Christ in one another. This made the most sense to me.

Regarding the question about what God was doing in all of this, He was showing me that His healing often comes through community. As we love one another in tangible ways, His lavish love is made known.

Chapter Fourteen

A NEW PACE

Father Stephen and his nephew were the first ones up the next morning. It was a little earlier than I normally got out of bed, but I knew I would be slow, so I joined them. I had told Rolando and the ladies to feel free to sleep in. Despite the long distance they had covered the day before, I knew their pace would be quicker than mine. They would easily catch up, so why not sleep in?

The three of us who were awake took our gear into the common area and began getting ourselves ready to head out. I massaged my ankle once more, wrapped it tightly, and gingerly put on my shoe. I thought, *Here goes nothing*, and asked God to give me the strength and endurance I needed to make it to Portomarin. The friend I was scheduled to meet would be arriving there in the evening. I had to make it there one way or another. I hoped and prayed it would be on foot.

Just before I left, I took a few moments to check Facebook and read several encouraging notes from people back home that had been thinking and praying for me while I slept. I was grateful for those who had been part of this journey, even though they were half a world away.

THE GOOD WAY

Holding on to what they shared, I stepped out into the street and onto the Camino.

I was the first one out of the albergue, with Father Stephen and his nephew right behind me. As they passed me, I asked Father Stephen to pray for me as I came to mind throughout the day. He assured me he would, offered a few words of encouragement, and walked off into the predawn darkness. I hoped the next five days of walking would bring me to Santiago. The Father was planning on being there in three—he had lots of ground to cover.

The street leading out of Sarria had a slight incline as it headed toward the monastery. This seemed to put less stress on my injury than walking on flat ground or going downhill. Not long after starting, the road turned to the left and steeply declined toward the edge of town. This caused significant pain. I attempted to adjust my stride so there would be less pressure and tension on the muscles and ligaments that had been sprained. It helped a little, but by the time I reached the bottom of this steep section, my hip was hurting. Compensating for my ankle put pressure on my hip. By the time I reached the bottom of this section, I thought, *If this is what my body feels like in this short distance, I'm not sure I am going to make it.*

The path leveled out and the pain in my hip subsided. I was left with the reality: The pain was consistent but bearable. Every now and then, I would step on a small rock or an uneven section of the path and would feel a twinge. Not even a kilometer into the day, and I knew it was going to be long and hard. I began to pray, "Lord, I need you, oh, I need you. With every step, I need you." I was taking a little creative license with Matt Maher's song, "Lord, I Need You." I did not think he would mind,

A New Pace

especially since repeating this prayer over and over again helped me push through pain and get into a rhythm of walking.

I would love to have had a miraculous healing from Helen's prayer the night before; instead, I was walking in pain, but at least I was walking. I thought of Paul's prayer for the removal of the thorn in his flesh. God answered, "My grace is sufficient for you." I then walked and prayed, "I need your grace. Thank you for your grace." I was not moving fast, but if the ankle did not get any worse, I could keep this pace up for some time.

Barbadelo was only about four kilometers from Sarria. I would use it as a gauge to tell me how fast I was walking. By the time I arrived, I realized I was moving at half the speed of my normal pace. To get to Portomarin, I would have to cover 22.4 kilometers. At my normal pace, with breaks, it would take four hours to make the journey. At my current speed, it would take me eight to ten hours to cover the distance. This seemed like a long day for an ankle that was recovering. I wondered what shape it would be in when I arrived. I pushed the thought out of my mind and returned to my prayer, "Lord, I need you, every step I need you."

There was a café bar in Barbadelo, and café con leche sounded good, but I knew it was going to be a lot longer day than normal, so I passed it by and kept walking. By now, I was wondering how long it would take for the Kiwis and Rolando to catch up with me. I did not know just how long they would sleep in, but if their pace was twice as fast as mine, they could overtake me at any time. A sense of anticipation was building inside of me. I looked forward to walking with them again, picking up where our conversations left off, and finding new paths on the

THE GOOD WAY

Camino and in our hearts to explore together. I hoped they would catch up soon.

Except for a stop to get a stamp in my pilgrim's passport and drink some water, I did not stop for the first twelve kilometers. I was afraid prolonged inactivity would cause my ankle to stiffen and make the afternoon harder than the morning. By the time I reached Morgade, I was hungry and tired. I had just passed the hundred-kilometers-to-Santiago marker and thought it was a good reason to celebrate. I stopped for a sandwich and a long drink of water. It was ten o'clock—I had been walking for four hours. My family had not caught up with me, but I was sure they would at any moment. I lingered there longer than normal, thinking they had to be just around the corner, but after forty-five minutes there was still no sign of them. Knowing that every minute I waited would make my long day even longer; I put on my pack and got moving.

The path leading away from the café was lined with a rock wall, and there was a small rock chapel just a few meters beyond the place where I had taken my break. I stopped to take a few photos and then continued on. Just a few more meters down the path and someone tapped me on the shoulder. A big smile swept across my face. I turned to see Helen and Amy. Their smiles were as big as mine. They told me Rachel and Rolando were just behind them and would catch up soon. In no time at all, they were there. All the questions and doubts of the morning were now washed away in the joy of the moment. We were now walking together once again. Having already covered more than half the distance, I was pretty sure I would make it to Portomarin. With my family at my side, I knew walking the rest of the way would be a gift.

A New Pace

We did what I hoped we would do. We picked up on old conversations and started new ones. It was wonderful to hear what their experience had been over the past few days and to share mine. As we walked, I could not help but thank God for the blessing of being able to cover the distance and the pleasure of doing it with these friends.

As we walked, I talked to Rachel about how at my normal pace I would have already arrived in Portomarin, but I would have sped past the beautiful country we were now walking through. "There are gifts to be seen in the hard places of life," I offered. "You just have to be willing to see them." I told her how all day long people would pass me and recognize I was struggling. They would greet me with "Buen Camino," and they would have compassion in their eyes. Some would speak to me in their own languages. Although I did not understand them, judging from their smiles and warm inflection, I knew they offered words of encouragement. Having seen my limp, I suspected they were thinking, *I am not sure he is going to make it. He needs to be encouraged*. To their surprise and mine, a little farther down the path, I would hobble past them as they took a break. We would smile at one another. With a couple of groups, this happened three or four times. Each time, the people seemed more optimistic about my progress, and in turn it made me feel more encouraged. While I did not know any of these people, their kindness toward me played a role in my ability to move forward. I would not have experienced any of this if I had not been injured and had been walking at my normal pace.

There were all kinds of gifts to be discovered. When I set out from Sarria, I had intentionally carried less water with me than I would have normally. A Nalgene bottle filled with water weighs about 2.75 pounds. I usually carried two. With my injury, I decided to forgo the weight, empty my bottles, and trust I would find water along the way. The pack felt lighter because of it.

When I set out from St. Jean Pied de Port, I was carrying the weight of the past two years of betrayal, hurt, and lost relationships. Over the past few days, as I waited for my ankle to get well, I had not realized that I was shedding these weights as I was experiencing God's compassion in the people he had surrounded me with. Like the water from my Nalgene bottle, it was as if I had left my deep hurts behind in Sarria as well.

As I walked alongside Helen and Amy, I felt lighter. The past and its pain seemed distant, and there was joy in the present moment. I was still walking with a limp, and I was pretty sure I would be for the rest of the journey, but I did not mind. I was happy to be walking and even happier to be in good company. I do not know exactly when the "bottle" that had been filled with hurt over the past two years was emptied, but I knew it had happened in Sarria. What had at first seemed like a trial to endure had become an opportunity for healing.

When I returned home from the Camino, I read a story Francis Chan shares in his book *Forgotten God*. It is about a group of South Korean missionaries—sixteen women and seven men—who had been abducted in Afghanistan. The Taliban held them hostage, and their kidnappers threatened to start killing them if their demands were not met. Over the next few weeks, two of them were killed. The rest endured hardship and harsh treatment before their release, but they also experienced God's presence and love in a powerful way. Francis tells of having dinner with one of these hostages, who shared with him the struggle of

A New Pace

coming back to their comfortable lives. As Chan relates:

> One of the most fascinating things this man told me was about what has happened since. Now that they have been back in Seoul for a while several team members have asked him, "Don't you wish we were still there?" He tells me that several of them experienced a deep kind of intimacy with God in the prison cell that they haven't been able to recapture in their comfort.

While I am sure none of them ever want to be abducted again, they do want to walk in the intimacy they shared with God while being held captive.

I would not wish a sprained ankle on anyone walking the Camino. If I ever walk it again, I hope I can avoid another injury, but I am thankful for the grace, love, and healing it brought to me. My Camino experience would have been less if it had not happened. I could not see it at first, but I came to recognize the injury as a gift.

The experience had forced me to rethink the past two years. What happened felt very much like an injury. Is it possible I could eventually feel about my emotional and spiritual wounds like I feel about my twisted ankle? I would still not call either experience good, but I would say they were opportunities for God to demonstrate His goodness. While I see it fully in my Camino experience, I am walking in faith that the same is true during this ongoing transition.

Sometimes I wonder if in five years—when I am settled into a new place in relative comfort—will I look back on this season and think, *I wish I could return there.* Will I long for how intently I looked for the presence of Christ in this time? Will I wish for the days when I found myself overwhelmed with gratitude for even the smallest gift God bestowed upon me? Will I remember how responsive I could be to the leading of the Spirit and long for the time when I had the freedom to do only what I see the Father doing? Will I remember what it felt like to be rejected and cast off and the fellowship with Christ this experience has allowed me to know? The apostle Paul put it this way:

> But whatever were gains to me I now consider loss for the sake of Christ. What is more, I consider everything a loss because of the surpassing worth of knowing Christ Jesus my Lord, for whose sake I have lost all things. I consider them garbage, that I may gain Christ and be found in him, not having a righteousness of my own that comes from the law, but that which is through faith in Christ—the righteousness that comes from God on the basis of faith. I want to know Christ—yes, to know the power of his resurrection and participation in his sufferings, becoming like him in his death, and so, somehow, attaining to the resurrection from the dead. (Philippians 3:7-11)

I had felt like I had been participating in Christ's suffering over the past two years. Walking on the path with Helen, Amy, Rachel, and Rolando, I now felt like I was getting to know in a deeper way the power of His resurrection.

We walked all together toward Portomarin. Unlike the morning, when I was worried about how long it would take to get there, I did not want the walking to end. We stopped at churches to take photos, sat on rock walls to

A New Pace

rest, and eventually took a longer break at a café. No matter how much I savored these moments, Portomarin was getting closer and closer. The final push to the city involves a steep downhill section, crossing a long bridge over the deep Mino Basin, and climbing a steep set of stairs that lead to the town. It felt like we had saved the hard part until the end, but it did not matter.

We had made it. I had gotten, by foot, from Sarria to Portomarin. I remembered how I felt on day three of the Camino, wondering if I had any hope of walking the full eight hundred kilometers. It seemed impossible. For motivation, I would imagine what it would feel like to walk into Santiago. It would be a joyful moment. Stepping onto the steep stairs leading to the center of Portomarin, I could have not felt any more joy. I imagined joy at completing the five-hundred-mile journey. In this moment, I experienced being completely filled with joy at being able to simply walk one more day.

By late afternoon, we were settled into our accommodations for the evening. The hostess at the albergue was kind enough to allow me to reserve a bed for my friend, who would be arriving later. We were now making plans for dinner. We had dreamed of hamburgers but ended up with sliced chorizo for our meat. Even so, with all the fixings and an appetite developed over hours of walking, it was delicious.

After dinner, we headed out to the city square to relax on the church steps, send a few messages back home, and wait for my friend to come. By 8:30, Jeff had arrived, and I was excited for him to meet my Camino family. I am sure it felt like a whirlwind for him as I introduced him to everyone and tried to give him a quick primer on what to expect for the rest of the evening and the next day. Once settled, I went with him as he grabbed a bite to eat at the café. When we returned to the albergue, we all gathered in the kitchen to cut up a watermelon for dessert. We invited anyone who passed by to join us. Some were brand new to us, others were those who had been walking with the Kiwis, the newest addition was my friend Jeff, and of course there was my family. It felt good for all of us to be together. It seemed a fitting way to end the day, celebrating the gift of being on pilgrimage and of community.

Chapter Fifteen

BLESSINGS

We had been walking for about four and a half hours when we stopped to rest at Ligonde. It was not the first stop of our day. Jeff and I had set out early, not knowing how fast I would be moving. I was sure the rest of the group would catch up with us rather quickly. It took at least an hour for my ankle to warm up, and then I could move at a decent pace. I felt bad for Jeff, a mountain goat of a hiker. Having hiked with him before, I knew he would be quick on the trail. I had told Tammie before my injury how excited I was to have my Camino legs because I felt like I would have a decent chance of keeping up with Jeff. Being injured, I was forcing him to walk at what must have felt like a snail's pace. Over the next few days, he would walk with me for the first hour or two. I would then tell him to move on at his own pace. It was his Camino too, and I did not want him to miss out on what it might hold for him because he was walking so slow with me.

While we walked together during the first hours of the day, I shared with Jeff what the experience of the Camino was teaching me and how the people I had met were impacting me. I told him about the people I had met in the beginning, my first Camino family, the life I found on the Masada, the loving-kindness of the Kiwis and Rolando, and about my friend Sergio. I could not wait for him to get to know some of them for himself.

I was excited to share with Jeff the morning ritual of café con leche at our first stop at Gonzar. It was only 7.8 kilometers outside of Portomarin, and it took us a little over two hours to get there. Because of my limp, we were not breaking any records, but I was making better time than yesterday. We stayed there longer than normal, hoping the rest of our clan would catch up. Just when we had given up hope and hoisted on our packs, I saw Amy walking toward us on the road. Soon, she and the rest of the group were at the café. We stuck around for a little longer, but began walking to get a head start. I was sure they would catch up to us quickly.

Two hours later, Jeff and I stopped for the second time at Ligonde. We were there just long enough to drink water and eat some fruit before the rest of the group arrived. Not only were Helen, Rachel, Amy and Rolando there, they also had with them Thomas from France, a woman I met for the first time at dinner the night before named Catherine, and Alice, the woman we had been walking with early on who stayed behind in Burgos. She had caught up to us in Portomarin, and was now walking with the group. I had thought I'd seen her for the last time in Burgos and now here she was once more. The Camino has a wonderful way of surprising you with people you did not expect to see again. It was good to have a friend from the beginning of the journey walking with us now toward the end.

While most of the group came and sat where we were, several went into the small albergue. When they came out,

Blessings

Rachel announced that her hip had been hurting and she did not think she could go on. She had checked and found that rooms were available. The Kiwis talked among themselves and decided they would stop. In just a few seconds, I understood we would be saying goodbye once again. My heart sank.

The others began to talk about what they would do, and one after another also decided they would stay as well. I could not blame them. It was a beautiful place. The albergue, which was run by a Christian order, offered a unique experience, and they had the time. Unlike Jeff and I, who had to be in Santiago by June 30 in order to catch a train the next day for Madrid, the rest of our friends had plenty of time to walk the Camino at a slower pace. Some even wanted to stretch it out as long as possible.

Rachel informed me of their decision. I told them I understood and thought they were making a good choice. Helen was already taking out a piece of paper and writing a note on it. Once she was finished, she joined Rachel and Amy as they came and gathered around me. Rachel pulled out a small item wrapped in white tissue paper and said they had something to present to me. It was a *pounamu* or greenstone. Rachel then read a blessing that is given with the stone. I learned that the *pounamu* is considered a *taouga*, or treasure, to the Maori, the indigenous people of New Zealand. It is a jade stone with spiritual significance. It is said each individual piece holds its own *mana* or integrity or strength. It is usually only received as a gift to affirm relationships, peace, love, and safe journeys. The stone came with a black strap to tie it around your neck, and I immediately put it on. Rachel said the stone chooses you and she thought the *pounamu* which had chosen me was a good one.

THE GOOD WAY

As Rachel spoke the blessing, some of us had tears welling up. After she finished, she looked in my eyes and said, "I hope you know you have also received three new daughters on the Camino." I said I knew it was true. Each one of them had carved their own place in my heart.

The moment felt exactly like what the stone is intended to communicate. It felt like an affirmation of the relationship we shared as family. It communicated the peace that we brought to one another and the love that had grown as we walked together. It also was a marker of our parting and the wish for safe travels for one another.

I had participated in blessings before. It is something we have intentionally incorporated into our family traditions. When I was responsible for overseeing the staff, I purposely created opportunities to bless and encourage one another. I know how empowering and affirming these kinds of moments are. The past couple of years of my life, however, had not always felt like a season of affirmation. This made the blessing the Kiwis bestowed upon me even more significant.

Blessing is most powerful when it is spoken in places of doubt, uncertainty, and waning confidence. I had been experiencing these for nearly two years. God's kindness to me has been consistent. He has brought people into my life to speak words of blessing and affirmation over me. Each one of these moments has been powerful. In seasons like this, words of blessing restore, build up, and bring hope. I felt these things as the Kiwis presented me with the *pounamu*. I was humbled to receive it.

We stood and embraced one another. I told them how thankful I was they came to me after I was injured, how their kindness had strengthened me, and how much I treasured each one of them. Helen handed me her note, she said she was not good at saying what she felt at moments like this, but wanted me to know what was in her heart. I did not need to read it—the tears in her eyes spoke volumes. I took the note and hugged them all one last time.

Saying goodbye to them the first time was difficult enough, and now it seemed even harder. I knew lingering would not make it any easier to walk away. I swung my pack on to my back and turned to leave. I said goodbye to Alice and told her how happy I was she was now with the Kiwis and then started to walk away. Thomas stood and asked if he could have a hug as well. Given our first meeting, I was surprised he would want to embrace an American, but was happy to hug him. When I turned down the path, I did not look back. My heart could not take it. I was afraid if I turned and saw them all standing there, I would not be able to go on.

Jeff was beside me as we walked away. He commented on the powerful moment that just took place, and then we walked in silence. I was quiet for the next hour. I thought about how I had walked away from Rolando and the Kiwis in Astorga, feeling as if God had used me to be an encouragement to them on their journey. As I left them in Ligonde, I could not help but feel I had been the one who received a blessing and encouragement through them.

It felt as if I had spent the first thirty-two days on the Camino surrounded by others; now it was just Jeff and I. Good company to be sure, but it felt a bit lonely to have just the two of us. I did not know what God was doing in all of this, but I was open to whatever was to come.

The remaining 10.3 kilometers we had to cover before arriving in Palas De Rei were mostly made up of paved roads meandering through the beautiful rural Spanish

THE GOOD WAY

countryside. The beauty was good for my soul; it reminded me there was still more to experience on this journey. It drew me into the practice of simply being present in the moment. I did not know what the final three days of walking would hold. I understood I could not keep the experience of the past few days from slipping into the past. All I could do was live in the present moment. There I could hold the sadness at having left my friends, enjoy the beauty surrounding me, and be open to what I might discover next. This seemed a good way to walk.

Walking in this good way did not change the fact that the last five kilometers toward Palas De Rei were the hardest of the day. Walking on the roadway caused the bottom of my feet to feel as if they were bruised. Each step brought with it a reminder of the soreness that was being pounded into them by the pavement. The good news was it took my mind off of my ankle and focused my attention elsewhere. By the time we arrived at the albergue, I was done for the day. I was physically spent, emotionally tired, and ready for a hot shower and rest.

The place we chose to stay was above a bar. We had run into a family just as we entered town that had told us they had heard good reports about the albergue, so we followed them there. After we all checked in, they were lead to the floor above ours. We were taken to a clean room with twelve beds, most of them empty. The only other occupant was a gentleman from France who did not speak any English. Since we did not know any French, all we could do was exchange pleasant smiles. While the accommodations were nice, three men in this twelve-bed room made me feel isolated.

It did not take us long to unpack our gear, take a shower, and wash our clothes. All the while I was thinking

Blessings

I needed to also prepare my heart. It seemed as if I was entering a new stage of the Camino, one that would be far different from what I had experienced earlier. I had learned enough along the way not to fight it. I was simply going to be open to whatever God would bring, even if it would be a greater sense of loneliness and isolation. I was grateful to have Jeff with me and was expectant to see how God would use this shared experience to strengthen what was already a strong bond between us.

Not long after we had taken care of our daily chores, the proprietor came back, this time with three college-aged women with him. We introduced ourselves and found out they were from Texas. Their names were Sidney, Alex, and Shaylee, two sisters and a friend walking the Camino together. Soon, we were swapping stories about our experiences. They asked about my ankle, and I told them the story of what had happened and the kindness my Camino family has shown me. Shaylee told us about a significant fall she had taken. Her hands were tucked into her pack straps and she could not break her fall. She landed on her head. She received scrapes, bruises, and maybe a mild concussion. She also received the kindness of people who came to her aid and cared for her. The compassion she was shown was one of the most significant experiences of the Camino for her. It all sounded very familiar.

One of the ladies who came to her aid handed her a crystal and told her to hold on to it. I am not sure what the lady thought the crystal would do, but for Shaylee it was a symbol of the loving-kindness of those who helped. She treasured it and said she would not give it away for anything. We made a game of trying to come up with something she might trade it for. We offered a million dollars. She thought about it for a minute and then said, "No." Regardless of what we suggested, she would not consider a trade. It was all good fun.

As I listened to other stories they had to share, I thought to myself, *Once again the space created by the separation from one family opens the space to embrace others.* I did not know if we would spend multiple days together or if this would be the one conversation we would share. I did, however, find myself simply being present in the moment and finding joy. It did not make me miss my Camino family any less, but it allowed me to be open to the reality another might already be forming.

This realization was one of the greatest blessings of the Camino: I could hold both the sadness of loss and the hope for what was to come as I lived in the present moment. I had recognized this earlier along the way, but coming back around to it helped to deepen and strengthen my heart's ability to live it. The experiences of the sadness of separation were like the yellow arrows along the Camino, as they pointed me in a direction I might otherwise have missed. They were way-markers that were helping me to recognize where I was headed. They were enabling me to find my way.

Chapter Sixteen

FINAL STEPS

I had thought the final few days of the journey might be different, and they were. We did not have the family group of eight to ten people surrounding us, but that did not mean we were alone. It also did not mean our current relational circumstances could not change.

The morning we sat out from Palas Del Rei, we ended up walking with a German couple Rachel had introduced me to in Portomarin. We were surprised to see them on the trail so early. They had told us the night before that they would be leaving around seven. It was only 6:30, and we were already walking together. They had heard it was going to rain and wanted to try to cover some ground before it began to fall. This couple had sold everything and decided to walk the Camino in hopes the journey would help them figure out what was next in life. They were walking with their three-year-old son. One parent would carry their backpack, and the other would carry the boy. I had a ton of respect for their willingness to walk the Camino with their son. Everywhere I ran into them, others were interacting and playing with their boy. He was like a magnet of joy for anyone who spent time with their family.

THE GOOD WAY

They were sharing with us the decision they had made, while walking the Camino, to move to India. The end of the Camino would only be the beginning of the journey for them.

Being early in the day, I was stiff and moving slowly. Before long, Jeff and the couple were walking a short distance ahead of me. I was glad Jeff had some people to walk with who could keep his pace. I was also happy he was getting to experience what it was to walk with others, hearing their stories and sharing his.

The threat of rain finally materialized in the form of drizzle, which in a matter of minutes developed into a downpour. People who thought the drizzle would dissipate and had not yet put on their rain gear were now stopping to pull out raincoats and ponchos. There is a bit of a dance that takes place, especially with ponchos, as travelers attempt to get them over their back and cover their pack. I had Jeff to help me with mine, but others were walking alone. We saw them flailing about, trying to get the waterproof fabric to fall over their pack. I would walk over and offer to help, pulling the poncho over their pack and smoothing it out. It was such a small act of kindness, but judging by the smiles on their faces, very much appreciated.

Other than these interactions, the rain seemed to have a quieting effect on conversation. You do not walk and chat like you might if it were a bright sunny day. The rain awakens your senses to the sound of it falling through the leaves and onto the path. You feel it against your skin and you smell it as you breathe. All of this quiets your speech as you settle into being present with the rain.

As I made my way through the morning, each step, interaction, and encounter with beauty was savored all the

Final Steps

more because I recognized I could have missed all of it. It was a gift to be continuing on despite my sore ankle.

By the time we reached the ten-kilometer mark, small rivers were forming on the path, and our feet were getting soaked. We spotted a café ahead that was filled with fellow pilgrims. We were happy to stop and join them, hoping that a short break would allow the worst of the rain to pass. Most of the people in the café were unfamiliar to me. Since travelers only have to walk the last hundred kilometers of the Camino to receive their Compostela in Santiago, many of them had started walking just a few days earlier. Most of the people seemed to be from Spain and spoke little English, if any. Still, we would greet one another with a friendly "Buen Camino" and a smile.

We had just about finished our café con leche when the Texans arrived. They had slept a little longer than we had, getting a later start. While their rain gear covered their upper bodies, they had already given up hope of keeping their shoes dry for the day. But their soaking-wet feet did not dampen their enthusiasm. We chatted a bit, wished them well, and headed out.

The rain did not last all day. By noon, the sun peaked out from behind the clouds. The rain had settled the dust and released the scent of the eucalyptus trees that lined much of the trail. I could not only see the beauty, but I could smell it as well. I was now moving at a decent pace. Jeff and I would walk beside one another for the next few hours, talking about the Camino and his observations after having been there only a few days. Jeff never had any longing to walk it. My desire to do so gave him an excuse to check off the last three countries he had not yet visited in Europe, so he asked to be able to join me at the end of my journey. As we talked, I could tell he was much more open to the idea of walking the whole Camino at some point in his life than he had been before. Even after only two days, he could see the draw it had on people and was starting to understand how it might fit into someone's life journey.

We wanted to spend our last night on the Camino in Monte del Gozo, so we would only have a short distance to travel on the morning we walked into Santiago. This meant we would have to walk longer distances over the next two days. We had decided to push past Ribadiso, which is where the guide recommended we stop, and head on to Arúza. We caught back up with the German family just before Ribadiso, where they would stop for the night. After parting with them there, we ran into a father and son we had heard about through Helen, Mark, and Sam. They were also heading to Arúza, so we walked together. Helen had walked with Sam at some point while we were separated and enjoyed their conversations. Meeting Mark and Sam was a matter of meeting friends of a friend, and so it was only natural we would be friends also.

We had more in common than just Helen, as it turned out Mark was a pastor as well. He asked me why I was walking the Camino, and I told him about the transition at my church, what the Lord was doing in me because of it, and how my journey was a physical experience of what I'd been processing internally and spiritually. He told me of his own difficult transition in ministry and immediately I knew he had been brought across my path for a purpose.

As we walked and talked, I discovered that Mark had, like me, done post-graduate work in spiritual formation. While we had never met before, we shared a common journey shaped by much of what we had been learning independently over the past decade. He knew people I knew and had been influenced by the Institute of Spiritual Formation, which is where I graduated from and now served as a spiritual director. It seemed with each step we took together, the world became smaller as we discovered the ways our lives and ministries overlapped.

I had spent much of the Camino walking with people who could be my own children. Now I was walking with a man of similar age, background, and internal makeup. It was probably what I needed most at this stage of the journey. As I was starting to process all I had experienced and felt along the way, I had someone walking beside me who knew better than most exactly where I was coming from. This in no way diminished the relationships that came before; rather, it rounded out the community that had formed around me. Karen had filled part of this role early on. Sergio certainly stepped into this gap as well. Now it was Mark's turn. While I had been consistently heard, loved, known and accepted all along the way, I now felt more fully understood. God's grace was surprising me once again.

I thought about how churches often build false walls between the generations. We segment people into ministries based upon their ages and life stages. In some ways this is reasonable, but there is also the need for spaces where all of the generations come together and grow to know one another. On the Camino, it is wonderful to have people from various generations sitting together around a table, after a long day of walking, and sharing life. It is great when nothing seems out of place when a twenty-three-year-old and a forty-nine-year-old can walk for kilometer after kilometer, talking about their relationship with Christ and helping each other grow in their faith.

THE GOOD WAY

Many of the false boundaries placed upon us by society and organizational structures, even within the church, are stripped away on the Camino. If you bring your authentic self, people are willing to enter into relationship with you no matter your age. Any barriers I experienced had nothing to do with age; they had to do with a willingness to be known. The extent to which people were willing was almost always connected to their capacity to trust. I could not determine if someone came to the Camino with this capacity intact. All I could do was take the risk myself and try to create an environment that invites others to risk trusting as well. Thankfully, the majority of people I walked with were willing to risk, and we all grew because of it.

Walking with Mark and Sam was another opportunity to trust, and I hoped our time together would last longer than the three kilometers between Ribadiso and Arzúa. Given the short distance, it did not take us long to arrive at our destination. Mark and Sam decided to stop at the first albergue in town; we joined them. We were in no hurry to complete our normal chores. The conversations we began on the road continued as we settled into the albergue.

Eventually, Jeff and I decided to go find a place to grab a late lunch. We lingered in the restaurant listening to bagpipe music, which is part of the culture of this Celtic region of Spain. Later in the evening, we joined Mark and Sam as they ate dinner. We sat at the table for a long time, sharing stories. They, like me, had traveled most of the Camino with a group of people who had become like family. For one reason or another, they also started to split up as they got closer to Santiago. You can hold off breaking up the family with the end still weeks away, but the closer you get to Santiago, the more the reality of

Final Steps

different schedules begins to intrude on the communities you have built. It is almost as if the world outside the Camino begins to squeeze itself back into your life. While this reality was affecting us all, it had not yet fully chased away the rhythm of our days.

The next morning Jeff and I left early, knowing my ankle would need time to loosen up. It would be our last long day of walking, roughly thirty-five kilometers. A little more than an hour into our day, we stopped for our morning coffee. I was excited to see a woman from Finland whom I had met earlier. The last time I'd seen her, we were sitting on a bench in a city park, taking a break. She was not going much farther that day, and I wanted to cover more ground. When I said goodbye back then, I thought it was the last time I would see her. Now here she was. Neither one of us could contain the smiles on our faces. She offered to share her table, and we spent the next thirty minutes catching up. She was going to take at least two more days to get to Santiago while we would arrive tomorrow. Seeing her was yet another unexpected gift.

By the time we had finished, Mark and Sam had caught up with us. We started out again together. Mark and Jeff walked ahead, and Sam stayed with me. He was a recent graduate from the Air Force Academy and would be going to his first duty assignment when this trip was over. He was young, fit, and fully capable of running laps around me as I limped along. I told him he did not need to stick with me, as I didn't want to hold him back. By now, Mark and Jeff were far ahead of us. He insisted on walking with me, saying he enjoyed the conversation.

We talked about life, faith, and dating. He explained to me what he studied in the academy and what his role in the military would be. We walked and talked like this for the next twenty kilometers. Walking on level ground or going uphill, I could keep a decent pace, but when we came to the downhill sections I would slow significantly. Sam would often make his way down these sections without me, only to wait at the bottom until I caught up. It was a great kindness he was showing me to keep my pace as we walked. It was another experience of someone simply being *with* me.

At this stage of the Camino, it felt as if we were walking in the rhythms we had been learning along the way. At the beginning, entering into these things often required a surrendering of your will and desires. Walking in them now seemed to come almost naturally. I could see it in myself and in my traveling companions. I have long heard that it takes thirty days for a new behavior to become a habit. It was day thirty-three on the trail. Maybe these rhythms were now habits. As I was experiencing what it was like to be walking in these new rhythms of life, my prayer was that they had indeed become habits of my heart.

Since we left the café in the morning, we had not stopped. Sam was sure his father would take a break at some point. Jeff and Mark were so far ahead of us that we could no longer see them. As we passed through the next few villages, we would stop long enough to poke our heads into the cafés and see if they were there. There was no sign of them. Finally, we found them sitting on some steps in Vilamaior. It was a Sunday and the whole town was out in the park just below the church listening to an orchestra play show tunes from American movies. Jeff and Mark had laid out a spread of fruit, cheese, and crackers, waiting for us to arrive.

We found a spot on the wall next to the steps and

Final Steps

enjoyed the concert as we rested our feet and fueled our bodies. Back home, we had often packed a picnic and headed off to a concert in the park to enjoy a similar experience. This was an unexpected surprise that filled me with the same sense of delight as those evenings in the park. A few minutes later, the three Texas women arrived. This was a surprise. They had passed us earlier in the day and we had not seen them again. We were sure they were in front of us. We invited them to take in the concert, and they accepted.

We could have sat there for a long time, and the rest of them lingered longer than I did. I was afraid my ankle would begin to stiffen up, so I told them I would start out and they could catch up. There was one last climb on the Camino as the road wound its way out of Vilamaior. As I made my way to the summit, I could still hear the band playing in the background. It seemed a fitting accompaniment to the last incline of the trail. I could not believe I had made it this far. I recalled the doubt of the first few days, and I remembered what it felt like to sit in Triacastela waiting for the bus, wondering if I would walk again. Walking had never felt so much like a gift. I could feel my heart pumping as I climbed. I allowed each beat to be praise to God for having allowed me to come this far.

It did not take too long for the rest of the group to catch up. We would walk the final few kilometers into Monte del Gozo together. Along the way, I was able to chat with Shaylee about what she would take home from the experience. She talked about the confidence she had gained in decision-making and in herself. She felt walking the Camino had changed her in a significant way. She talked about how she imagined this would affect her life and relationships at home. While she shared, I thought, *I*

THE GOOD WAY

think it had shaped all of us in significant ways.

Mark had shared with me earlier how he felt the experience of the Camino would affect the way he shepherded and ministered to people. He was thinking about how he could incorporate the rhythms he had learned while walking in his community of faith back at home. He wondered if people would be able to fully understand what we had experienced and how much life flows out of it. He also shared how the Camino had been teaching him to be fully present with people when they were near and how to hold them loosely, knowing in the next hours, days or weeks, they might move on. My experience on the Camino affirmed what he was sharing. We share our lives in the moment; sometimes these moments last longer than others.

At Monte del Gozo, you catch your first glimpse of the city of Santiago de Compostela and the spires of the cathedral. It is also the home of a large complex built in 1993 for the benefit of pilgrims, with more than five hundred beds. I had no doubt we would be able find a place to sleep. What did surprise me upon our arrival was how empty the place felt. It was like a ghost town, but this was easy enough to overlook. We were only an hour's walk from completing our journey. The complex was made up of multiple bungalow-style buildings. Each had a long hallway that stretched the entire length of the building. On either side were rooms housing eight beds each. The seven of us ended up taking one for ourselves. We would spend the last night before Santiago as a family.

We were pleased to find there was a kitchen at one end of the building and decided to make a meal together. I was happy Jeff would be able to taste what had been such an important part of the experience of walking the Camino.

Final Steps

Mark volunteered to make us pasta the way Beppe had shown him. The Texans suggested we combine the alfredo and red sauce that was available at the local tienda into one concoction. They had been told by other pilgrims it was good and thought we should give it a try. We did, and it was. I offered the corkscrew from my Swiss army knife and helped with cleanup. Everyone pitched in where they could. We had added a salad to our entrée, yogurt for protein, and a couple of chocolate bars to split for dessert. Meals on the Camino are bit of a hodgepodge, based on whatever ingredients are available. It makes the meals more interesting, and the process of preparing them more fun.

We toasted one another and getting to this point on the journey. We broke bread together, enjoying our last meal on the Camino before Santiago. During and after dinner, we continued the conversations we had been weaving in and out for the past few days. It felt very much like a family dinner. I thought, *This is my third Camino family*. I was happy to have discovered one, was surprised to have found a second, and was now enjoying the company of a third.

I was excited to walk into Santiago in the morning, but part of me did not want this evening to end. After dinner, we explored the large complex. We were also on the prowl for Wi-Fi. There was one spot in the center of it all where you could access the Internet for free. Before heading back to our room, we stopped to check our smart phones for messages from home. When I scrolled through Facebook, I saw a post from Rolando. He was still with the Kiwis and the others we had left behind in Morgade. They had to be at least a day behind us, maybe more. His post declared, "Tomorrow I arrive in Santiago." If this were true, they would be arriving sooner than expected. Could it be possible I would see them again?

A smile came across my face as I looked up from my phone. The complex was empty, except for our little band of explorers. There was stillness over the compound and in my soul. I drank in the golden light of the setting sun, which bathed the walls of surrounding buildings. I allowed myself to envision walking into Santiago with these people in the morning. I also permitted myself to hope of the possibility of being reunited with Rolando and the Kiwis. My heart filled with joy at the thought of it. Knowing tomorrow would be a gift, I headed back to my room.

Chapter Seventeen

SANTIAGO

We were so close. We knew in just a few minutes we would be standing in front of the cathedral. Mark, Sam, Jeff, and I had come into the city together. With the excitement of almost being there, our pace had picked up. We were focused on the markers leading the way, so we did not notice Mark's friend sitting in a café we had just passed. This was someone Mark and Sam had walked with for much of the Camino. The man jumped from his seat and came rushing out into the street calling Mark's name. He had not expected to see this friend again, and Jeff and I watched as the men embraced. Smiles filled their faces at the joy of seeing each other. Introductions were made and then Mark and his friend spent time catching up. The chance meeting was an unexpected surprise—it set the tone for the day.

There was a bounce in Mark's step as we continued on. I think all of us felt it. There was an expectation building for what the day would bring. We made our way up the Rúa das Casas Reais, across the Praza de Cervantes, down the steps and through the arch that led into the plaza in front of the cathedral. It was still early, and there were very few people there. It was as if we had the place to ourselves. For a moment, we just stood and looked at one another.

In that moment, I forgot about the five hundred miles I had walked over the past month. I did not notice the stiffness in my ankle. I simply felt the joy of having arrived. Along with the joy came a sensation that we had entered rest. We now had nowhere else to go; we were there. This realization painted smiles on our faces that said everything. We gave one another big bear hugs and slapped each other on the back. It was the next best thing to pinching ourselves to ensure we were not dreaming. While I am sure it would have been wonderful to have all of our friends with us at that moment, there was something sacred about the empty plaza, the quiet of the morning, allowing us to soak in the moment. We lingered there for a while, took some photos to remember our moment of arrival, and eventually got around to planning our morning.

The Pilgrim's Mass would be at 11:00 a.m. We did not know if they would be flying the Botafumeiro, the giant swinging metal container—or censer—that burned a combination of coal and incense. It has been swung in the cathedral since the twelfth century as a way to freshen the air that was often filled with the smell of recently arrived pilgrims. The ritual is generally performed only on Fridays and feast days. They will also fly it on other days if there is a group willing to pay the cost.

We decided to be there early to get a seat just in case. Before then, we would find a place for breakfast, store our packs at the storefront that provides the service, and explore the interior of the church. With no pressing agenda, we were soaking in the experience of being

Santiago

present in Santiago.

With a little over an hour before mass, we found seats in the front row in the right transit. It would be a perfect spot should the Botafumeiro be included in the mass. We took turns visiting the crypt of St. James and climbing the stairs to an area behind the altar to embrace the saint's gilded statue. While taking in the beauty of the cathedral, I discovered the Texans had made it as well. They were sitting in another section of the church. They told us where they were staying. We decided after mass to grab our packs from where they were stored and see if we might get a bunk there as well. It was nice to know we would all be together.

Returning to my seat, I sat watching familiar faces go by. Some of the people I knew by name, and we greeted each other warmly. Others I recognized but without names to go with faces. I had walked alongside of them, shared a room with them, and even brushed my teeth next to them. But because of language barriers, we had only exchanged smiles. I wanted to hug each and every one of them. As they passed our seats, we would look into one another's eyes and exchange a knowing glance and call out, "Buen Camino." We had shared the experience of struggle and hardship. We had persevered together, offering encouragement as we went, even it if was only through a smile or small act of kindness. We now shared a sense of joy and accomplishment at having arrived, which formed a bond between us.

The church quickly filled up, and judging from the flurry of activity, it was a good bet the censer would be included in the service. I asked one of the security guards if they were going to fly the Botafumeiro. She smiled and said it was possible. With anticipation building, people

THE GOOD WAY

were now being directed to sit on the floor. Ropes were being put into place to keep people from crossing the path where the censer would swing.

Before long, the clergy made their way to the altar. Among them was Father Stephen, our companion for portions of the trek, which made the service more personal. I was excited for him and thankful to share the experience.

Each Pilgrim's Mass began with a reading of the number of pilgrims who received their Compostela the day before, a certificate of completion written in Latin that confirmed the completion of a pilgrimage undertaken for religious devotion, and the names of the countries they were from. It was amazing to sit there and think that millions of people have made this pilgrimage over the centuries, and we joined the multitude of pilgrims who ended their journey by coming to this place of worship.

Early in the service, eight men dressed in burgundy robes began to prepare the Botafumeiro for the ritual of swinging it through the sacred space. Father Stephen joined them, adding incense to the hot coals that the attendants had placed in the censer. The eight men then began to rhythmically pull on the rope. At first, the censer was lofted straight up into the air and fell back down toward the altar with little sideways movement. The men timed their pulls for just the right moment to turn the vertical motion into horizontal energy. The large silver-plated brass censer began to swing from side to side. The men then began to time their pulls to cause the Botafumeiro to ascend to the ceiling of the cathedral. Soon it was flying past our heads in its arc toward the heavens. It was a holy moment. Music played in the background, the scent of the incense began lofting over us, and I began to lift up praise to my heavenly Father for the grace He had shown me on my journey. I thanked Him for the people who had supported me back at home, for those I had walked with, for being able to complete the journey to Santiago, for the struggles along the way, and for this beautiful experience of watching the Botafumeiro swing gracefully through the air.

Almost immediately after the service, we started to bump into people we did not expect to see. Jay and Deb were the first to make contact. The last time I had seen them was in Sarria. They were delighted I had made it, confessing they did not think it would happen. When we turned around Madu, a man from India who had been sharing the Camino with us ever since Portomarin, was standing there with his Compostela in hand. We also gave each other a big hug and celebrated making it to the end. This scene repeated itself over and over again, like a big family reunion. I had expected to see the people I had been walking with over the past few days, but I was surprised at how many I was running into from the early days. Many heard through the grapevine that I had twisted my ankle and had been praying for me or sending well wishes my way. The delight on their faces at seeing me in Santiago was a gift.

As the day progressed, it seemed that each time we turned a corner there would be another person we knew and another joyful reunion would ensue. Eventually, we found the albergue and checked in before we retrieved our packs. Before we went back, we stopped at the market to buy food so we could make a picnic lunch in the square. We retrieved our packs and found a spot where we could watch all the reunions taking place in front of the cathedral. With nowhere to go, we had no reason to hurry.

THE GOOD WAY

Each time a group would enter the square, we would share in their excitement. Often they would stop to take photos or embrace others they knew. There was laughter and tears of joy. We would go and greet people we recognized. Otherwise, we sat back, eating the delicious food laid out before us, delighting in the celebrations which were on display.

Eventually we made it to the albergue, one of the nicest I had stayed at. Mark decided to stay there and spend time meditating on what completing the journey had meant to him. Jeff went off to arrange a car to take us to Finisterre the next day. Sam agreed to go with me to purchase souvenirs to take back to my family.

Somewhere along the way, I received a message that the Kiwis and Rolando would be arriving in Santiago around 2:00 p.m. Now 3:00, we headed to the square, finding no sign of them. They had given me the name of the albergue where they were staying, but when we checked there, they had not arrived. Our next guess was the Pilgrim's Office, so that is where we went next.

Turning the corner into the courtyard of the office, we immediately saw Helen, Rachel, Amy, and Rolando at the front of the line. The German couple was there as well. So were Alice and Catharine. I was almost to them when they turned around and saw me. Tears immediately started flowing down Helen's face. She said she did not know if she was going to see me again, and here we were. We hugged and expressed our gratitude at once again being together. Sam and I waited until they had received their Compostela. We took a group photo to commemorate the moment and then agreed to meet for dinner. We had already invited our third Camino family, and now many of our second would be there as well. The day was getting better and better.

The Kiwis, who had made reservations at another albergue, agreed to meet at ours by 7:00 p.m. for dinner. They were running late. Fearing they might have gotten lost, I began to circle around the Cathedral looking for them. I turned a corner and there stood Brant, someone I'd not seen since day six or seven. He had left the Camino for a few days for a side trip and had been walking behind us ever since. I was happy to see him because we had not exchanged information. I did not even know his last name. Now, I could be sure to get the information necessary to keep in contact. Most of the people he had walked with had already departed, and he was already missing the community of the Camino. He was planning on spending the next year traveling and did not know how different it would be from the experience of walking The Way. We spent a few minutes talking and encouraging each other and then exchanged contact information. We embraced and said our goodbyes. I went back into our albergue to see if I might get on the Internet and connect with the lost group. As I was logging on, I looked up and saw them standing outside the window.

We headed over to the restaurant across the square and joined the others. There were thirteen of us in all, and another ten I wished could be there. I looked around the table and was so grateful we could share this meal together. I also realized we might never eat together like this again. I determined I was going to make the most of it. I would speak words of affirmation and blessing to each person as time and space would allow. Throughout the dinner, we weaved in and out of pockets of conversation along the length of the table. When it seemed appropriate, I would turn to an individual and share what I had seen in them, what I discovered about who they were, and what I believed about who they could become. If we never saw one another again, I wanted them to know how much I valued each of them.

I thought about how rich the experience of this meal felt, and I wondered why we do not share these kinds of moments more often back at home. While I am not sure anyone understood in the moment I was speaking blessings over them, I could see in their faces how impactful it was to their hearts. A tear would come to their eyes, a smile would form on their face, or they would offer a sincere thank you in response to my words. In turn, they would often offer a blessing to me. I wondered what it would be if we made speaking to one another like this in our normal life a part of our regular routine. Scripture instructs us to do so: "Encourage one another daily and build each other up" (1 Thessalonians 5:11). This is part of what it looks like to live in biblical community. We were experiencing it in a palpable way as we sat around the table. Because you never knew if you would see someone again as you walked, blessing one another was a virtue we had been learning to exercise along the way. At this meal, we were seeing it expressed in its fullness. It was beautiful and life giving. I desired for this practice to be something I would not leave behind in Santiago.

Only the curfew of the albergue kept us from continuing the conversation until late into the night. We said our goodbyes. Mark and Sam would be going with us in the morning, but for the rest of them this would be the last time we would see them here. I agreed with the Kiwis not to say goodbye again (this would make the third time) but to simply say, "Until we meet again." We had learned from all the reunions of the day that God would bring back around to one another those He intends. The change in how we expressed it did not erase the realization that this would be the last time we were together for some time, maybe forever. It took a while to complete all the hugs and speak our last words to one another. It started in the restaurant and spilled out it to the street. A light rain helped to move things along, and before we were completely ready, we were walking in separate directions heading back to our albergues.

As I lay in bed, the memory of each reunion I experienced throughout the day replayed itself in my mind. I did not want to sleep for fear that when I awoke I would not remember as clearly each meeting and conversation. The day had been far richer than I had imagined it could be. Walking into Santiago carried with it a joy all its own, but it was the reunions with people that had made the day so special. As I thought about each interaction, I thanked God for the people and what they had meant to my journey. Each person had carved a place in my heart. I knew I would be carrying each one back home with me.

* * *

The next day, we planned to rent a car and drive out to the lighthouse in Finisterre, a place people once believed to be the end of the earth. We had agreed to meet Annemarie the next morning in the plaza in front of the cathedral. She was waiting when we arrived. Thirty-five days earlier she and I had set out together from St. Jean. Along the way, I had taken several photos with her, thinking it might be the last time I would see her. I was thankful to be mistaken. As we stood there waiting for Jeff to bring the car around, I

THE GOOD WAY

asked her to take one more picture. I handed my camera to Sam and stood next to her. She was one of the first persons I walked with on the Camino and now she was the last person I would stand with in Santiago.

Chapter Eighteen

GOING HOME

Jeff's flight left several hours before mine. This left me sitting at the Madrid Airport at 5:30 a.m., long before I need to be there. Ticketing would not open until 7:00. Once the ticket agents started to roll out the signage and queue dividers, people gathered in line. As we waited for ticketing to open, the airline began to take our passports and prescreen us for security. When the agent came back with my passport, he informed me that my flight had been delayed by several hours and asked me to leave the line so they could process those on earlier flights. This was a problem. I would not be able to catch my connecting flight if I was delayed for several hours. When I pointed this out to the agent, he directed me to the customer service window. It did not open for another half an hour. I refused to let this inconvenience steal from me the peace I had gained on the Camino. I turned to God and prayed, *Father, I will simply trust you in this situation. I am willing to be open to whatever you are doing.*

Fortunately, I was the only one in line at customer service. Unfortunately, the posted time for opening came and went without any sign the darkened office would soon be occupied. One person did open the door at the back of the small room, raising my hopes, only to turn on the lights and just as quickly turn them off. "I am willing." I repeated to the Lord.

Not long after my momentary hopes had been dashed, an airline ticketing agent came and stood beside me outside the window. She too seemed to be hoping to find some help inside and seemed frustrated at the lack of personnel in the darkened room. I asked, "Are you having a good day?" She responded that it is too early to tell. "Well, then," I said, "if it is not bad yet, chances are it will be a good day." A smile came over her face. She then asked why I was standing at the counter, and I told her how my flight had been delayed, which meant I would not make my connecting flight.

With great determination, she said, "Follow me." She proceeded to walk me to the front of the line I had been asked to leave. She said something in Spanish to the ticketing agent, who pointed back to the people waiting in line and replied to her in a stern voice with words I did not understand. My new acquaintance did not look pleased with the answer. She turned back to me and said with even more firmness, "Follow me!"

I did not know what she had in mind, but I knew she was intent on making something happen. She opened up another terminal and asked me where I was headed. "Los Angeles," I said. After many clicks on the keyboard and a bit of wrestling with the printer, she handed me a boarding pass that routed me to my destination through a new city. When I looked at the connecting flight, I realized I would actually arrive home three hours earlier than my original flight. God is good.

Going Home

* * *

As I settled into my seat, I recognized the lady next to me. She and her family had been standing in line in front of me before I was asked to step aside. She was alone. Her children were scattered in seats behind us, and she told me her husband did not get a seat on the flight. He worked for the airline, and they had all been flying standby. I did not have the heart to tell her I think I took his seat. But she was not worried—he would catch the next flight, the one I was originally booked on. I then fessed up and told her I had originally been on that flight, and it had been delayed so I was bumped to this one. They were used to traveling on standby and having to be flexible. She was sure they would meet up later in the day. With that, we retreated into silence.

I was thankful. I had planned to use the hours of flight time to process what I had experienced on my journey. I pulled out my journal and began to flip through the entries I had made along the way. I also began to write down important details I had failed to include—the names of people I'd met, the countries they were from, places I'd stayed, and other details. I knew it was important to write down as much as I could while it was fresh in my mind.

I turned to thinking about the themes that might grow into chapters. I started to jot down titles that would help me remember what I was thinking. They were far different from the list I had set to paper before I had departed. People would ask me before I left home, "What is the book going to be about?" I would have to answer, "I don't know." I wanted to hold it all loosely and allow the journey to surface what God had been doing all along. I felt like an expectant parent who had not found out the baby's gender. Only labor and delivery would reveal what God was forming and shaping internally.

I remember what it was like when our first child was born. While we knew he was going to be a boy, we did not know what he would look like, how he would sound when he cooed and cried, or what it would feel like to hold him. We were filled with wonder when he arrived. We were also filled with a bit of shock when they sent us home. We were being handed a significant responsibility—but they did not even give us a test or an interview to make sure we were ready. We did not feel ready, but it did not stop them from handing us the baby and saying, "Here you go."

I had the same feeling as I sat there thinking about what I would write about. I had gone through labor and delivery, I was filled with wonder at what had been born, but I was not sure I was capable of caring for it. I put the journal away and simply began to thank God for what He had been teaching me over these past two years and how I had seen these things expressed on the Camino.

The great temptation of this entire journey was to try and determine what the end would be before I took a single step. What I have discovered both on the Camino and in this transition is it is not about the destination, it is about who you are becoming. Who you become will determine where you will go. Despite my desire to do so, I cannot control my circumstances. This is a blow to the ego. We all want to feel as if we have control over the circumstances of our life. The reality of living in a fallen world smashes this illusion. There is so much in life that is beyond our control. We cannot control if we will be laid off, get cancer, have our spouse choose to leave us, find out our child is using drugs, or experience the sudden loss of a loved one. We may try hard to make sure none of these happen to us. We may stay late at work, eat all the right foods, read all the marriage books, build walls of protection around our children, and beg God in prayer to heal those who are sick. All this does is produce anxiety and cause disappointment when we find our best efforts are not enough to keep us from the pain and hurt we feared. Jesus made it very clear when He said, "In this world you will have trouble" (John 16:33). Trying to avoid it or insulate ourselves from it is a losing battle, one leading to the sense that we have failed or that God has failed us. This leads us to despair.

Jesus also commands us in the same verse, "Take heart." He has overcome the world. Standing at the crossroads, we are not to seek to control our circumstances or find our comfort in being able to identify a destination. We are to turn to Him in trust, knowing He has overcome it all. This is a hard move to make, but in doing so we are lead away from anxiety and into peace.

I carried a guidebook with me as I walked the Camino. It was helpful, but the maps contained on the four-by-eight-inch pages could in no way illustrate the land we would walk across as we covered fifteen to twenty miles per day. The truth is, I could have easily made the journey without it. All I had to do was follow those who were walking before me and watch for the yellow arrows and shells that marked the way.

I remember leaving Pamplona in the predawn hours. The way-markers were hard to see. A couple stepped out of a hotel in front of me and turned toward the Camino. They walked with confidence, as if they had traveled the path before. I gave up looking for signs and simply followed them. They led me out of the cluttered city and into the countryside where the way was easily discerned.

THE GOOD WAY

I did not determine which direction to turn at the crossroads because I was able to see the destination clearly. I determined the direction to walk by following Christ. When I follow Jesus, I am lead to humility, submission, surrender, waiting, forgiveness, trust, authenticity, and love. To follow in this path requires the stripping away of anything that may hinder me for walking in them. This is hard. At times, the cost can feel unbearable. A willingness to follow Him into these things leads to life—the abundant life Jesus said He came to give us. I tasted abundance as I have walked along the dusty paths of the Camino.

As I sat there thinking through these things, I turned and looked at the woman sitting next to me. I thought about the series of events that led me to occupy seat 12D. The person I was five or ten years ago might not have found himself sitting in this place. He would have responded much differently to being asked to step out of line because his plane was delayed. He would have tried to control the situation. He would have shifted into assertive mode and demanded something be done to ensure he was going to catch his connecting flight.

I had watched someone respond exactly like this the summer before. I was traveling the country, installing phone systems and found myself in Atlanta. There had been a big thunderstorm in the area that delayed flights in and out of the airport. My plane was late arriving, which caused me to miss my connecting flight. I stood in line with scores of others who needed to find a way home. The person in front of me was heading to the same city as I was. I listened as she talked to the agent behind the counter, hoping to hear what our chances might be of getting home.

As she talked to the agent, she became more irate and

her tone of voice became more condescending. It was apparent she was not getting what she wanted. I thought this did not bode well for me. I could see the veins on her neck begin to bulge as she became more and more frustrated. I could also see the effect it was having on the airline worker, who was also looking frustrated.

Listening in and watching what was taking place, I resigned myself to the fact I would not be getting home that night. I started to ask God to show me what He might be doing. I also decided I would not add to the "whipping" the customer service representative had already received. When it was my turn to approach the desk, I simply said, "Rough day! I'm sorry you have to be the lightning rod for people's frustrations." She looked up and made eye contact with me. Smiling, she asked, "Where are you headed?" I told her my destination. She clicked through a few screens, typed on her keyboard, and then handed me a boarding pass. I was on the next flight.

This was but one of the experiences God had been using over the last few years to teach me to trust Him, even when the circumstances seemed out of control. My journey on the Camino seemed to be an opportunity to exercise what I had been taught. I was literally walking in all that God had been forming in me internally, relationally, and spiritually. Rather than pressing the assertive button in Madrid, I was content to wait and see what God might be up to.

I cannot say I was free from all anxiety and stress. I wanted to get home, and I knew my Spanish was nonexistent. I wondered how I would communicate what I needed. Each time these feelings would surface, I would turn my heart back to God and ask for help in trusting what He was doing. This was a lesson I had been learning for almost a decade. The past two years of transition caused me to increase my exercise of this discipline, and the Camino was an experience of walking in this good way. I felt like I was continuing to walk in it even as I was making my way back home.

When I arrived home, a friend of mind told me she knew I would finish the Camino, even after I was injured, because she knew I liked to conquer things. She knew I would not allow anything to keep me from finishing. When she said this to me, I thought, *She's remembering who I was before this transition, before I walked the Camino, before I had learned to wait.* She had no way to know how content I was as I walked away from Astorga with what I had already learned. At the time, I really felt like if my journey ended right there, it would have been complete. The prospect of not finishing showed me there was still something deep inside me that wanted to make it to Santiago, but it had nothing to do with conquering the Camino.

I finished the Camino de Santiago because I had, as one of my fellow pilgrims had so poetically put it, entered the current of the Camino. He said people come to the Camino and they either learn to allow it's current to carry them along or they swim against it, wearing themselves out in the process. It is like floating in a moving river. It feels unnatural at first. Your body wants to react to the motion and lack of control by flailing your arms and legs, or giving up the attempt at floating altogether and flipping over and swimming. This, of course, takes more energy and tires you out quickly, especially if you are swimming upstream. It can also cause you to sink.

It took a few days to quit flailing about on the Camino. It is hard to release control and enter a state of rest, allowing the water to hold you and the current to carry you. This can only be accomplished with an active intention to not flail but float. Walking like this on the Camino was a tangible physical experience of the active waiting God calls us to embrace as we learn to trust and follow Him.

My response to being asked to leave the line at the Madrid airport was a direct result of having learned what it is to trust, wait, and rest. This is different from who I used to be. I could see the change, and I knew this was what coming to the crossroads was all about. Who I am becoming will determine where it is I am going.

As we approached Newark Airport, I turned to the woman next to me and asked if she would be willing to allow me to use her phone to contact Tammie when we landed. I explained I had no way of letting her know I was arriving earlier than expected. She was happy to oblige. Once the plane touched down and we began taxiing to the gate, she turned on her phone. She began to receive a series of text messages from her husband, who had been left behind in Spain: "Honey, I got on the next flight. . . . We are boarding the plane. . . . We are sitting on the tarmac. . . . We've been delayed. . . . The pilots have now passed the number of hours the FAA allows them to be on duty in a day and must return to the gate. . . . No other flight crew is available. . . . Going to a hotel for the night—will try to catch a flight tomorrow."

After she finished reading them out loud, I said I was sorry it had not worked out. She said, "It's okay. He'll figure something out." She then handed me the phone, and I sent Tammie a text. I was surprised at how well the woman sitting next to me took it all. With a husband who was employed by the airline and as a family who regularly flew on standby, they had gone through this before. It was almost expected.

I had been away from home long enough and my heavenly Father knew it. He also knew the plane would not only be delayed, but cancelled, and He provided me with a way home. My part in the process was to wait by the counter, respond with kindness to those He brought across my path, and trust that He was up to something in the midst of the circumstance. I was keenly aware of how gracious God had been to me to bring that particular airline worker to the counter at just the right moment. The experience reminded me that my heavenly Father knows the most intimate details of my life and understands what I need. Having sent the text, I sat there in confidence, knowing if God cared enough to provide me a flight home that He would also lead me where I needed to go.

I handed the phone back to the woman. A smile came across my face and a feeling of contentment washed over me. God had invited me to seek the ancient path, the good way. Now, having learned to recognize it and walk upon it, my soul was indeed at rest.

Epilogue

REST ASSURED

It took nearly a month after arriving home for my ankle to heal enough for me to walk again. During the recuperation period, I simply allowed the experience of the Camino to soak into my soul. The day I resumed my daily walk through Hartwell Park was also the day I sat down to begin writing this book.

To focus my thoughts before writing, I would walk through my beloved park and pray about where to start. Often, I would arrive home with the first paragraph written in my head. Much like the shell markers or yellow arrows on the Camino, this would give me a direction to head, but it did not allow me to see the next turn until I arrived at an intersection and spotted the next arrow. The writing process seemed to be an extension of my journey on the Camino. When finished, I was surprised to realize it had taken the same number of days to complete the book as it did to make my way to Santiago. This all seemed right, even poetic, and I wondered if this chapter of my life was now closed.

Within a month of finishing the book, I returned to my former church for the first time since I had left. The leadership had let go of a worship leader who had served that body for more than forty years. My wife and I wanted to attend his final service to honor him. I remember walking excitedly up the steps into the sanctuary the morning of his farewell. I had not seen many of these people for well over a year. The awkwardness and uneasiness I am sure would have remained months earlier was now gone. All I felt was delight. The morning was filled with big smiles, warm embraces, and the opportunity to encourage one another as followers of Christ. My wife and I lingered long after the service to reconnect with people. I had the opportunity to sit beside those I dearly love, look into their eyes, listen as they shared, speak words of encouragement, and tell about my recent journey. It was a gift born out of my walk on the Camino.

During this same month, the man who had served as elder chairman for most of my time at the church entered the hospital for back surgery. The operation went well, but during his stay he developed a life-threatening lung infection. Except for one brief conversation, I had not spoken with his man—my longtime mentor—since being let go from the staff. Our once-close relationship had gone silent. I had no idea if he would recover, but I knew I did not want our friendship to end with the awkward silence that had dominated the last year and a half.

Even though he was on oxygen and having difficulty breathing, he was coherent when I arrived at his hospital room. I stood by his bedside and told him how much I had appreciated all that he had poured into my life over the years and how much of my leadership development could be traced to his mentorship. We did not speak of my dismissal or the subsequent silence. It did not seem necessary. Looking into his eyes, I knew we both understood the significance of the moment. My mentor took my hand and held it with his strong grip for a long time. There was no awkwardness in the quiet we slipped into. It was filled with peace. I knew, even if he would not recover, something was healed at that moment.

In the course of my visit, I learned my mentor had known that the longtime worship leader was going to be let go and had gone to him to share what was coming. Some faulted him for this. I saw it as evidence he was still growing in his understanding that the church was not a business, but a family and needs to be led accordingly. The lack of this kind of candor and caring had led to the silence between us. I was encouraged to know that in a similar situation, he had made a different decision. Perhaps, the words I had spoken to him on the morning after I was laid off had not fallen on deaf ears.

A few weeks after the hospital visit, we all gathered back at the church for his funeral. It was a service led by former staff and elders. I was honored to speak on behalf of this man. Six months earlier, I could have not imagined it. At that time, my heart would not have been able to speak the truth of his life, the experience of his leadership, and how he had been used by God to shape me. I could participate in the memorial service because of what God had been teaching me while walking in the Camino's good way and the clarity it brought.

One of the people asked to speak at my mentor's service was a former elder who had recently been removed from the board. He was released in part because of his role in sharing the plans for dismissal with the pastor of worship that would be affected. Not long after the service, I received a text message asking if I would meet with him.

THE GOOD WAY

When we got together, the former elder said he and his wife felt as if their time at the church was coming to an end. He knew that several of us were seeking God's leading about forming a new faith community, and he wanted to know if they would be welcome.

In a strange turn of events, I found myself sitting across a table from one of the men who had voted to remove me from the only ministry I had ever imagined myself serving. Looking into his eyes and hearing his story, I knew he was hurt. Even more, I knew exactly what he was feeling, because I had experienced much of the same hurt and rejection. It is in moments like this you choose how you will walk. Will you choose to allow the hurt you have experienced to determine your course, or will you choose to walk in the freedom of the good way? The simple phrase "Free people, free people" flashed in my mind, and I knew in an instant the way I would choose to walk. I told him he was more than welcome to become part of our community, and while I had no idea how long he and his wife might stay, I hoped they would find it to be a place of healing.

The path God leads us on is often surprising. In my wildest dreams, I had never imagined this conversation would take place. But now that it did, I could envision that this former elder's presence in our new community would bring further reconciliation and restoration. I had come to another crossroads, another arrow pointing the way. Now that I could see it, I simply had to walk on the path and trust God to continue to lead.

To live like this is to enter into rest. When we think of rest, we typically imagine taking a break and ceasing activity for a specific allotment of time. The kind of rest we are invited into, however, cannot be quantified by time or measured by inactivity. When God invites us into rest, He calls us into a state of being, a way of living rooted in dependence and trust in Him. This kind of rest allows us to love our enemies, forgive, release, wait, and move forward, even when we do not fully comprehend where He might be leading. It also gives birth to peace, contentment, and joy. So I encourage you to "stand at the crossroads and look; ask for the ancient paths, ask where the good way is, and walk in it," because I have discovered it is there "you will find rest for your souls."

¡Buen Camino!

Appendix

THE SIGNIFICANCE OF THE CAMINO DE SANTIAGO

The Camino de Santiago, or Way of St. James, is a pilgrimage route to the Compostela de Santiago in Northwestern Spain. Traditionally, a pilgrim would begin his journey at his doorstep. This explains why there are many routes that cross Europe and Spain, all considered part of the Camino de Santiago. When people refer to the Camino, however, more than likely they are referring to an eight-hundred-kilometer path (five hundred miles) that stretches from St. Jean Pied de Port, France, to Compostela de Santiago. Known as the Camino Francés, this route crosses the Pyrenees, travels through the Meseta (or flatlands), and then climbs through the beautiful green hills and mountains of Galicia.

People have been traveling this path on pilgrimage for more than thirteen hundred years. It was the discovery of what many believe to be the bones of St. James, a disciple of Christ, which made this a significant place for people of the Christian faith to travel. James had preached the gospel in the region before returning to Jerusalem, where he was beheaded by King Herod Agrippa. It is said that his bones were returned to Spain, where they were eventually rediscovered and enshrined in Santiago. The first record of people making the pilgrimage dates to the ninth century. By the twelfth century, the Camino had become a well-organized and well-traveled pilgrimage route. Making the journey to Santiago became one of the three important pilgrimages during the Middle Ages, the other two being to Rome and Jerusalem. Of these three, only the Camino remains intact and widely traveled today.

While millions of people have been walking to Santiago since the Middle Ages, in 1985 fewer than one thousand people made the pilgrimage. In 2014, the year I walked the Camino, almost 238,000 people received their Compostela, a document that has been given to those who have completed the pilgrimage to Santiago since the early Middle Ages. Those who made the journey and then told their stories encouraged this resurgence. When German celebrity Hape Kerkeling published his book *I'm Off Then: Losing and Finding Myself on the Camino de Santiago*, German people began to show up in great numbers. The number of people from Korea who make the walk has also been steadily increasing, due in part to a television documentary that aired in their country a few years back. Credit is also given to the translations of Paulo Coelho's book *The Pilgrimage* into the Korean language. While I walked, I heard many locals comment on the increasing numbers of Americans who make the pilgrimage. I am sure the 2011 movie *The Way* has much to do with the renewed popularity.

More than anything, I believe people are drawn by the longing for community and meaning, the desire to lay down their burdens and the need for rest. These have been placed in our hearts by our Creator. If my story has stirred these in you, I would encourage you to look

Appendix

through the following resources, which helped me along my way. It might be time for you to make a pilgrimage of your own.

- *A Pilgrim's Guide to the Camino de Santiago* by John Brierley
- The American Pilgrims on the Camino: www.americanpilgrims.com
- Camino de Santiago Forum: www.caminodesantiago.me

¡Buen Camino!

NOTES

Chapter 10, Wilderness and Stones

p. 114   Timothy Keller, *The Meaning of Marriage: Facing the Complexities of Commitment with the Wisdom of God* (NewYork: Riverhead Book, 2013), p. 101.

Chapter 14, A New Place

p. 165   Francis Chan, *Forgotten God: Reversing Our Tragic Neglect of the Holy Spirit* (Colorado Springs, CO: David C. Cook, 2009), pp. 107-108.

ABOUT THE AUTHOR

Ronald K. Ottenad is an Adjunct Professor at Talbot School of Theology at Biola University. He also serves as a Staff Spiritual Director at the Center for Spiritual Renewal, in La Mirada, CA. He is the founder of Rooted Soul Ministries, which seeks to create environments where people can encounter God and learn to walk in freedom. He served as a pastor in a large church for 21 years and is currently partnering in planting a new church. He has a Bachelors of Arts Degree in Journalism from California State University Long Beach, and two Masters of Arts Degrees from Biola University, Organizational Leadership and Spiritual Formation and Soul Care. He has been married to his wife for 28 years and has two children.

www.ingramcontent.com/pod-product-compliance
Lightning Source LLC
Chambersburg PA
CBHW051648040426
42446CB00009B/1031